MW01047235

The Truth Shall Make You Free Devotional

What God can do for You
What You can do for God

Bible Verses with Words to Comfort and Inspire You

PAVERS
Publishing

The Truth Shall Make You Free Devotional™
Published by Pavers Publishing, LLC
28211 Southfield Rd., #760152, Lathrup Village, MI 48076
www.PaversHomes.com

ISBN 978-1-938989-07-0
ISBN 978-1-938989-08-7 (electronic)

Copyright © 2013 by Pamela Osborne

Scripture quotations are taken from The Holy Bible, King James Version

Book cover and page design by Shannon Crowley,
Treasure Image & Publishing – TreasureImagePublishing.com

Editorial development by Minister Mary D. Edwards,
Leaves of Gold Consulting, LLC – LeavesOfGoldConsulting.com

Published in the United States of America by Pavers Publishing, LLC.
Printed in the United States of America

10 9 8 7 6 5 4 3 2 1

SPECIAL SALES
Most Pavers Publishing, LLC books are available at special quantity discounts when purchased in bulk by corporations, organizations, and special-interest groups. Custom imprinting or excerpting can also be done to fit special needs. For information please email info@pavershomes.com, or call (248) 809-5121. More Pavers Publishing, LLC books can be found at www.PaversHomes.com.

Acknowledgements

I'd like to acknowledge God for all His goodness toward me. Without Him, this book would not have been possible. With Him, I have peace and love. Thanks to Him, I also have forgiveness. I also want to thank my family and friends for their words of encouragement.

I thank my editor, Minister Mary Edwards of Leaves of Gold, LLC, for her wisdom. I also thank Rahijaa Freeman of Creative Buds Inc., for her creative, business and marketing acumen.

The book is dedicated to all of the oppressed people in the world, whether physically, mentally, or spiritually.

Introduction

*Return to thine own house, and shew how great
things God hath done unto thee. And he went his
way, and published throughout the whole city how
great things Jesus had done unto him.*

*40 And it came to pass, that, when Jesus was
returned, the people gladly received him: for they
were all waiting for him.*

Luke 8:39, 40

In *The Truth Shall Make You Free Devotional*, author, Pamela Osborne wants to share these "good news" verses in hopes that they will be uplifting and inspiring to you as you travel this world. We may not understand everything that happens to us, but we can trust in God who does understand. He will work things out according to His purpose. By the way, His purpose includes His love for us. This book's devotionals will comfort and inspire you to pave your life with a purpose, by serving God who blesses you every day of your life.

The Truth Shall Make You Free Devotional focuses on joyful, comforting and peaceful verses. They cover the rewards of being a Christian. It's what Christians shout about! God guarantees you freedom, happiness, contentment, joy, peace of mind and eternal life, IF you believe Him to be your Savior. As you read the verses and devotionals, think about the many blessings and how well God has equipped you to succeed in whatever His purpose is for you.

The Truth Shall Make You Free Devotional also covers God's instructions to us on how to be a good Christian. The essentials of being saved by Christ are few: believe that Jesus is our Savior sent from God and confess our sins. However, we show our belief in Christ by being doers of His Word. They will focus on some very significant instructions, which can help you to see what actions you can take as a Christian. Although a few

7

passages cite what not to do, the vast majority of verses cite positive avenues for constructive action as a Christian.

Daily reading of the Holy Bible has many benefits. It can bring joy and comfort. It provides timely instructions in directing every facet of your everyday life, big and small. Nothing is too little or too large for God to handle. It helps you to practice more naturally the will of God. This is one of the ways God communicates with you.

A suggested way to read *The Truth Shall Make You Free Devotional* is to sit quietly and read just one per day. Feel free to look up in your Bible additional scriptures related to these for a deeper understanding. Reflect how they apply to you and help you through your daily living.

Enjoy God's Gifts to You!

SOMETHING TO SHOUT ABOUT!

Blessed be the Lord, who daily loadeth us with benefits, even the God of our salvation. Selah.

He that is our God is the God of salvation; and unto GOD the Lord belong the issues from death.

Psalm 68:19-20

Every day, the Lord blesses you with loads of benefits. These benefits include the "motherload" of benefits: salvation and eternal life. Whoa! Think about that. No other "god," and I use that term loosely, because there is only one God, who can promise and deliver that. That's worth a shout. Halleluiah!

COUNTING YOUR BEAUTIFUL BLESSINGS

And God said, Let us make man in our image, after our likeness: and let them have dominion over the fish of the sea, and over the fowl of the air, and over the cattle, and over all the earth, and over every creeping thing that creepeth upon the earth.

So God created man in his own image, in the image of God created he him; male and female created he them.

And God blessed them, and God said unto them, Be fruitful, and multiply, and replenish the earth, and subdue it: and have dominion over the fish of the sea, and over the fowl of the air, and over every living thing that moveth upon the earth.

Genesis 1:26-28

Before salvation and eternal life, we had to be created. And God got creative! Scientists have barely scratched the surface of understanding and identifying all of the things that God has created. Because of God's decision, you and I can enjoy a beautiful physical world that He has created for our benefit.

How many specifically listed blessings can you count in the above three verses?

1. He made man
2. He made female
3. He gave human beings the authority to be fruitful and multiply and replenish the earth (also known as sex)
4. He blessed us
5. He made us in His likeness

6. He gave us power/authority over:

    a. The fish of the sea

    b. The fowl of the air

    c. The cattle, and

    d. Every creeping on the earth

7. He gave us the power/authority to subdue the earth.

This world was created for our enjoyment. People were created by God in a way that gives us countless benefits that we can enjoy every day of our lives, such as a beautiful sky, a green garden, and soothing, flowing waters. It didn't have to be that way. He didn't have to put us in charge of so many things. God just loves that way.

FOOD FOR THOUGHT

And God said, Behold, I have given you every herb bearing seed, which is upon the face of all the earth, and every tree, in the which is the fruit of a tree yielding seed; to you it shall be for meat.

And to every beast of the earth, and to every fowl of the air, and to every thing that creepeth upon the earth, wherein there is life, I have given every green herb for meat: and it was so.

And God saw every thing that he had made, and, behold, it was very good. And the evening and the morning were the sixth day.

Genesis 1:29-31

What is your favorite food? Praise God, we are not stuck with just eating hay and water all of our lives. Sometimes we get stuck in a routine of eating the same kinds of things day in and day out. If it is well balanced, fine. But for those of us who want to try something different every now and then, there are, literally, thousands of food items to choose from. There are meats, fish, seafood, and poultry. There are herbs and other parts of vegetation used as medicine to keep us healthy. There are natural ingredients to keep us clean, beautiful and smell good. From sweet to sour, and from crunchy to soft, there is a food to satisfy every taste and human need. Now bless your food.

DELIGHTFUL DAYLIGHTS

*And the LORD smelled a sweet savour; and the
LORD said in his heart, I will not again curse the
ground any more for man's sake; for the
imagination of man's heart is evil from his youth;
neither will I again smite any more every thing
living, as I have done.*

*While the earth remaineth, seedtime and harvest,
and cold and heat, and summer and winter, and
day and night shall not cease.*

Genesis 8:21, 22

Many years ago, God became sad over the wickedness He saw in mankind's behavior. So He cursed the earth and flooded it (the whole thing!), destroying every living creature and vegetation, except for what was on Noah's Ark. After the Great Flood of Genesis, God again blessed the earth, by promising that as long as the earth existed, there would be seeds planted and there would be harvest time. There would be seasons for cold and hot weather, like the summer and winter. Daylight would be followed by nighttime.

There is comfort in knowing that God made a covenant with Noah and mankind that He would not flood the earth like He did in Genesis ever again. I have heard of people, upon landing from a long airplane trip, kissing the ground that we all take for granted from time to time. So next morning when you wake up, hopefully, from a good night's sleep, enjoy your daylight, because it is a blessing from God.

NEW LIFE, NEW BEGINNING

And God blessed Noah and his sons, and said unto them, Be fruitful, and multiply, and replenish the earth.

And the fear of you and the dread of you shall be upon every beast of the earth, and upon every fowl of the air, upon all that moveth upon the earth, and upon all the fishes of the sea; into your hand are they delivered.

Every moving thing that liveth shall be meat for you; even as the green herb have I given you all things.

Genesis 9:1-3

Imagine this: everything on earth was destroyed by God in a flood, except what was saved on Noah's boat. Granted, it was a very big boat; but even that alone couldn't have replenished the earth like we see today without God's blessings. What God took away, He can bring back. It is good to know we can all have a new beginning with God. Our past does not have to condemn our future. I like an old saying my mother used to tell me when I was going through some tough times. She would say, "It will pass. It won't last forever." No matter how bad you think you were, God can give you a new life, a new you.

GOD'S RAINBOW PROMISE

And I will establish my covenant with you; neither shall all flesh be cut off any more by the waters of a flood; neither shall there any more be a flood to destroy the earth.

And God said, This is the token of the covenant which I make between me and you and every living creature that is with you, for perpetual generations:

I do set my bow in the cloud, and it shall be for a token of a covenant between me and the earth.

And it shall come to pass, when I bring a cloud over the earth, that the bow shall be seen in the cloud:

And I will remember my covenant, which is between me and you and every living creature of all flesh; and the waters shall no more become a flood to destroy all flesh.

Genesis 9:11-15

Aren't rainbows pretty? There is something about seeing a rainbow shining through a cloud after a rain. Who else but God could have thought of something that only He could give as a gift to us?

He promised not to flood the earth again to "perpetual generations." There is something in legal terms that is referred to as "the rule against perpetuity." It means that courts frown upon contracts that are binding "forever" from generation to generation, with no end in sight.

Fortunately, God is not limited by man's laws. His promise to us was not only to prevent a world-wide flood, but, if you caught the benefit of the above sighted verses, there will be generations after generations who will be blessed by this beautiful world He created.

Stop what you are doing sometimes, and think about how God delivered on His promise to you and all of your relatives. Be reminded of this every time you see a rainbow.

HOW GREAT LOVE IS

For God so loved the world, that he gave his only begotten Son, that whosoever believeth in him should not perish, but have everlasting life.

For God sent not his Son into the world to condemn the world; but that the world through him might be saved.

He that believeth on him is not condemned: but he that believeth not is condemned already, because he hath not believed in the name of the only begotten Son of God.

John 3:16-18

John 3:16 is one of the few verses I memorized as a child and never forgot. God can relate to us. He has a Son that He sent to war, to sacrifice His life to save ours. Who could question God's love for us after all that? Everlasting life is the ultimate gift that God has done for us. Sometimes it is tempting to think, with all of the bad things that are happening around the world, that God may not love us. But when you go back to John 3:16-18, He assures us that it is not His desire to condemn the world. Everyone who believes that God sent his ONE AND ONLY SON so that we can be saved knows that God is a loving God...a good God. There has got to be a better way for people to get along with each other, and God has shown us that way through His Son, Jesus Christ.

THE GIFT OF EVERYTHING

John answered and said, A man can receive nothing except it be given him from heaven.

John 3:27

We can't do anything without gifts from God. We can't breathe, wake up, go to sleep, get dressed, eat, work, play, have fun... nothing, nada... zip... zero. That is why we should thank the Lord for, as the old saying goes, "Waking us up this morning, and starting us on our way."

Sometimes, we can get "big headed" and think we "did it all by ourselves, with no help from anyone." Maybe you have thought that no human has helped you; but even that is humanly impossible, when you think of the condition you were in as a new born baby. God certainly had not only helped you, but helped you every year, month, day, hour, minute, second, and nanosecond (i.e. a billionth of a second) of your life. Next time you take a breath, let it out with a "Thank you, Lord."

TRUE FREEDOM

Then spake Jesus again unto them, saying, I am the light of the world: he that followeth me shall not walk in darkness, but shall have the light of life.

And ye shall know the truth, and the truth shall make you free.

They answered him, We be Abraham's seed, and were never in bondage to any man: how sayest thou, Ye shall be made free?

Jesus answered them, Verily, verily, I say unto you, Whosoever committeth sin is the servant of sin.

And the servant abideth not in the house for ever: but the Son abideth ever.

If the Son therefore shall make you free, ye shall be free indeed.

John 8:12, 32-36

"Freedom" can mean a lot of different things. One can be free from housework, free to eat anything you want, free to go anywhere you want and freedom from slavery. Jesus was talking about spiritual freedom. The Son of God made us free from sin. That is the truth that shall set you free. It is not free to hurt someone, or free to be irresponsible. It is free to do the right thing, free to love, and free to not be tied to the sins of the past. That is true freedom.

WHAT'S YOUR NEIGHBOR'S GIFT?

For I would that all men were even as I myself.
But every man hath his proper gift of God, one
after this manner, and another after that.

I Corinthians 7:7

God has given people different gifts in order to best serve Him. As Christians, we should have an understanding of what our gifts are. There are books on spiritual gifts that may be helpful to you finding out more about such gifts.

Gifts were not meant to exert any superiority over others with different gifts. Each one serves a vital purpose for the unity of saints. What are the gifts of the Christians around you? How can all of us work together to maximize the service to others and improve our own development?

HE CAN WORK IT OUT

Likewise the Spirit also helpeth our infirmities: for
we know not what we should pray for as we
ought: but the Spirit itself maketh intercession for
us with groanings which cannot be uttered.

And he that searcheth the hearts knoweth what is the
mind of the Spirit, because he maketh intercession for
the saints according to the will of God.

And we know that all things work together for
good to them that love God, to them who are the
called according to his purpose.

Romans 8:26-28

There are days when you may not know if you are coming or going. Your "to do" list appears to be a "can't do this" list. There are situations that you may find yourself in that you just don't know, not only what you want, but also have no idea on how to get it. It can be like walking through a thick fog, where you cannot see across the street, but you know you can't stand still either. You know something is on the other side of the road, but the only way to get there is to trust God to get you safety to it.

That is where the Holy Spirit comes in. The Spirit can guide you safely through the fogs of life. It would be so much more comforting, you think, if you knew all the details of your journey... or would it? I believe that there are reasons God does not reveal our whole life to us in advance. One of which is to learn to trust Him. The other is that He knows how much we can bear. Whatever the reason in your situation, I know that He can work it out, because *"all things work together for good to them that love God." (Romans 8:28)*

OUR FATHER

*For ye have not received the spirit of bondage
again to fear; but ye have received the Spirit of
adoption, whereby we cry, Abba, Father.*

*The Spirit itself beareth witness with our spirit,
that we are the children of God:*

*And if children, then heirs; heirs of God, and
joint-heirs with Christ; if so be that we suffer with
him, that we may be also glorified together.*

Romans 8:15-17

I like to think that this is especially for the fatherless, the
rejected child of a father, the abused and neglected, those who
have disappointing "father figures," and those abandoned by
their father. Even those who have or had loving fathers know
that our earthly father will not always be with us. There is a
void when the reality of life without a physically, mentally or
emotionally present father hits us. For me, because I had a
loving father, it hit me upon his death. Even though I was
grown and had a family of my own, I just didn't realize the
physical loss of my father would hit me so hard emotionally.
Nevertheless, I found great comfort that my heavenly Father,
allayed all of my fears about my loss. I found out through the
Holy Spirit that I have a heavenly Father who not only takes
care of me, but also takes care of my earthly father in heaven. I
believe that they are both looking on my life and wishing me
well. There is peace in knowing Daddy is okay. Everyone can
have a great, wonderful, loving Father. Our heavenly Father has
said that we are His children. He will never leave, reject, abuse,
neglect, disappoint, nor abandon us.

YOUR NOT-SO-PERFECT GIFT

When they (the wise men from the east) saw the
star, they rejoiced with exceeding great joy. And
when they were come into the house, they saw the
young child (baby Jesus) with Mary his mother,
and fell down, and worshipped him: and when
they had opened their treasures, they presented
unto him gifts; gold, and frankincense and myrrh
(fragrances). And being warned of God in a dream
that they should not return to Herod, they
departed into their own country another way.

Matthew 2:10-12

During the Christmas season, for those who practice giving out and receiving Christmas presents, ever wonder what kind of gift you will receive this Christmas? Will it be something pretty, practical, or excitingly entertaining? Will it be big or small? Will it be cheap, chic, or dripping in cash? Did you get exactly what you wanted when you opened up your gift on Christmas day?

On the other hand, do you have the task of shopping and looking for that perfect gift for a love one? Face it. Some of us are very hard to shop for. There are so many things to choose from. The range could be from homemade, dollar store, gift cards, to a new car, or house. How do you pick the perfect gift, within your budget, of course?

Picture this. God is up in heaven, looking down on earth at His children. Many have been waiting for centuries in anticipation for the Messiah to come. God had to decide when, where and how. After all, there was never a Christmas before. Lots of details had to be in place, including the big star in the East so that the wise men could find baby Jesus. Then in the whole wide world, God had to pick the blessed parents, and explain what was going to happen.

God pulled it off by giving us the perfect gift of Jesus Christ

23

on that first Christmas Day. It's okay if your Christmas gift does not top that. The wise men's gifts were given from the heart with love. God looked out for the protection of the wise men as they journeyed back to their homes. Any gift you give on Christmas, if given in love, and not-so-perfect as Christ, will be made perfect in God's sight.

DIAL "G.O.D." FOR RELIEF

The Spirit of the Lord GOD is upon me; because
the LORD hath anointed me to preach good
tidings unto the meek; he hath sent me to bind up
the brokenhearted, to proclaim liberty to the
captives, and the opening of the prison to them
that are bound;

To proclaim the acceptable year of the LORD, and
the day of vengeance of our God; to comfort all
that mourn;

Isaiah 61:1, 2

This prophecy in Isaiah of the coming of the Messiah, foretold what Christ was going to do for the meek, brokenhearted, and captives. Christ gives us good news in a bad news society, mends broken hearts, frees us from all kinds of captivities created out of our circumstances, real and imagined, and opens the doors of inner and outer imposed prisons.

Some people try to find "relief" from a deep hurt through drugs, drinks, food, sex, immersion in work, or excessive TV distractions. Then one day when they "give up" trying to handle their grief on their own, either they turn to God, or God shows pity on them and sends them a sign or guardian angel to deliver them up out of their despair. Whatever you are mourning about today, seek God's comforting words and wisdom. Just call on His name, wherever you are, and you will not be disappointed because **God Offers Deliverance.**

PICTURE THIS

For the mountains shall depart, and the hills be
removed; but my kindness shall not depart from thee,
neither shall the covenant of my peace be removed, saith
the LORD that hath mercy on thee.

O thou afflicted, tossed with tempest, and not
comforted, behold, I will lay thy stones with fair
colours, and lay thy foundations with sapphires.

And I will make thy windows of agates, and thy gates
of carbuncles, and all thy borders of pleasant stones.

Isaiah 54:10-12

You can't say, "God isn't visual," through Isaiah's prophecy. What a picture. Imagine mountains falling into the sea from a ferocious volcano. Imagine that familiar hill you used to climb back home is now gone from a sunk hole. Then, seemingly out of nowhere, Christ appears with a just-what-you-need act of kindness and peace. Imagine that you got caught up in a sudden and unprecedented storm, and the car that you are riding in is tossed to and fro. But, somehow, you land safety on a street paved with brilliant precious stones of turquoise. Your new home's foundation is built with sapphires and rubies. You look over and see your home's windows framed in agates (a semi-precious stone of various colors), and the gates leading up to your house are of carbuncles (a shiny red garnet-like gemstone). Your yard is bordered in curb appeal stones that the best decorator in the world couldn't have conceived.

Will heaven look like this? Will the earth? It is hard to imagine all of the wonderful things God promises us, even when we, like Israel, have been very bad. God forgives. Just to show what it truly means to forgive, He promises blessings beyond our imagination.

HE'S GOT YOUR BACK

*And all thy children shall be taught of the LORD;
and great shall be the peace of thy children.*

*In righteousness shalt thou be established: thou shalt
be far from oppression; for thou shalt not fear: and
from terror; for it shall not come near thee.*

*Behold, they shall surely gather together, but not by
me: whosoever shall gather together against thee shall
fall for thy sake.*

*Behold, I have created the smith that bloweth the
coals in the fire, and that bringeth forth an
instrument for his work; and I have created the
waster to destroy.*

Isaiah 54:13-16

Don't mess with the Lord's children. I think of God's power whenever I start to be concerned about others' political, police, and bully powers. I will do my best to defend and protect myself. After all, God gave me a brain to use for my safety. However, there are some, actually many, actually most, things out of my control. I could fret and worry and lose sleep over them, or I could be reminded of the passage above. Anyone who attempts to hurt me shall fall at the Lord's hand.

Is there someone that you are fearful of? Do you worry about "what's going to happen next?" Give your fears and troubles to God. He can do what you cannot do. He can send guardian angels to keep you from the intended harm of others. He is the ultimate destroyer of evil and the protector of good. So the next time you look over your shoulder, believe God's got your back.

LOOK STRAIGHT AHEAD

No weapon that is formed against thee shall prosper; and every tongue that shall rise against thee in judgment thou shalt condemn. This is the heritage of the servants of the LORD, and their righteousness is of me, saith the LORD.

Isaiah 54:17

Life is like being pregnant. Once you are born and living through the various stages of life, there is no turning back. Like pregnancy, in which either you are or you are not, you can't be half dead and half alive. Either you are going somewhere on this journey, called life, or you are no longer alive. So there is no turning back. You have to walk through some pretty scary passages of life. You can't say, "Okay, I messed up my teenage years. Let's go back and do that again."

So when you face the inevitable challenges in life, most of which you have never faced before, otherwise, it wouldn't be a challenge, you need to know that God has seen it all, even before you knew it was coming. One of the things He wants you to remember in your "once-in-a-lifetime" existence is that not only will He protect you, He will provide the ultimate social justice, the "final disposition" in a court of righteousness, and the "fair punishment" to people who want to hurt you.

As comforting as that might sound, that should not be the focus of your thinking. Keep moving toward your goals and purpose. If He wanted you to have 360 degree vision, He would have given you more eyes that could see all around you at one time. Like pregnancy, you should think positive thoughts and stay calm. Expect a happy outcome. Yes, God knows people may not like you because you are black, white, yellow, brown or red, too fat, too skinny, too pretty, too ugly, too rich, too poor, too smart, and/or too dumb, so they may want to hurt you. Nevertheless, look forward, and let God handle the darts and arrows. Let God love you and protect you, just as you are. You've got a dream to birth, places to go, and things to do. There is no turning back. Look straight ahead and push toward to your blessings.

YOU ARE TOUCHED

But the Lord is faithful, who shall stablish you,
and keep you from evil.

And we have confidence in the Lord touching you,
that ye both do and will do the things which we
command you.

II Thessalonians 3:3-4

Ever gotten an unexpected touch on the shoulder? You look around and see a dear friend who happens to see you from way across the room. What a warm and comforting feeling if it is someone that you like and admire. Or sometimes you are touched on the shoulder by a stranger who politely informs you that you inadvertently dropped something, like a glove, scarf or hat.

The Lord has touched you to remind you that He is your friend that noticed you from anywhere you are in the world. He reminds you in so many different ways that He is there, faithfully looking over you and protecting you from evil. He also reminds you to do good things that he has politely informed you to do. Be open and receptive to the hand of God.

KNOCK, KNOCK

And I say unto you, Ask, and it shall be given you; seek, and ye shall find; knock, and it shall be opened unto you.

10 For every one that asketh receiveth; and he that seeketh findeth; and to him that knocketh it shall be opened.

Luke 11:9, 10

Life is so uncertain. Who knows what the next day, or minute will bring? As human beings, we want to know if we open a door, what is on the other side. Well, we may not know a lot of things, but one thing we do know. If we knock on Christ's door, He will answer. Yes, He answers our prayers. And we also know that we may not get everything we ask for in the way we expect. I like to think that He knows what we are really asking for, in the spirit, and does what is best for us, even if we do not understand the uncertainties of life. In reading Luke 11:1-13, Christ emphasizes that a friend who knocks on your door asking for bread, would get bread, if he had it. A friend would not turn a friend away. Christ goes on to say that if man, being evil is so hospitable, how much more likely it is for Him, who is good, would give the Holy Spirit to those who ask for it. The Holy Spirit can tell us what we need to know for our good, when we need to know it. So knock away and seek knowledge, understanding and wisdom. Your heavenly Father has good things for you behind your door.

DELIVERED

Notwithstanding the Lord stood with me, and strengthened me; that by me the preaching might be fully known, and that all the Gentiles might hear: and I was delivered out of the mouth of the lion.

And the Lord shall deliver me from every evil work, and will preserve me unto his heavenly kingdom: to whom be glory forever and ever. Amen.

II Timothy 4:17, 18

Have you been through a very harrowing, and downright traumatic experience? Have you been so down that you didn't know which way was up? Most people have. Also most people recover. The Lord will stand by you in your desperate hour of need. He will strengthen you. Imagine looking in the mouth of a lion, and being delivered from a painful ordeal. The Lord can deliver you from every evil thing that you can imagine. He can save you from your enemies, drugs, alcohol, financial disaster, lost loved one, broken dreams, everything and anything. Yes, pain and death is inevitable. But God can deliver us and preserve His heavenly kingdom for us. The pain and challenges of life sometimes can only be handled by knowing that we have a Savior who can deliver us from all evil.

WAIT UP

When the poor and needy seek water, and there is none, and their tongue faileth for thirst, I the LORD will hear them, I the God of Israel will not forsake them.

Isaiah 41:17

God will not leave you. He is there to give you everlasting water to quench your soul of thirst. He is as essential to your well being as the water from a well. You really can't live well without Him. We get behind in partaking of our spiritual nourishment, just like we often neglect to eat our fruits and vegetables. But have no fear, God is patient. He will wait for you. Just say, "Wait up, Lord, here I come." Don't worry. He will be there.

COME EMPTY - LEAVE FULL

*...Every one that thirsteth, come ye to the waters,
and he that hath no money; come ye, buy, and eat;
yea, come, buy wine and milk without money and
without price.*

*For ye shall go out with joy, and be led forth with
peace: the mountains and the hills shall break forth
before you into singing, and all the trees of the
field shall clap their hands.*

Isaiah 55: 1, 12

When things seem at their lowest, God seems to step in.
There is always hope with God. Never give up your dreams,
your mission, and your purpose. Where there is God, there is a
way. It is not how much you own that makes you valuable, it is
how much you believe in God's love for you and His desire to
help you fulfill your purpose. Do you want to feed the hungry
children in Africa? You can. Do you want to save lives in bullet-
ravaged inner cities? You can. Do you want to comfort the sick
in nursing homes? You can. Do you want a better life for you
and your family? You can, do all these things through Christ.
He empowers us to be what we were meant to be: kind, loving,
giving, and sharing. But first, He knows you come with
nothing. He knows you thirst and are hungry. He knows you
need money and an uplifted spirit of joy and something to sing
about. So you come to Him, empty, down, rejected, hurt; and
you leave full of joy and peace of mind. He rewards you with
love, so that you can shout to the world, "WHAT A GREAT
GOD!"

YOU WAIT, WHILE GOD WORKS

*He giveth power to the faint; and to them that
have no might he increaseth strength.*

*Even the youths shall faint and be weary, and the
young men shall utterly fall:*

*But they that wait upon the LORD shall renew
their strength; they shall mount up with wings as
eagles; they shall run, and not be weary; and they
shall walk, and not faint.*

Isaiah 40:29-31

Many times we are asked to set five and ten year goals, which is a good thing. However, try looking back five and ten years. Where were you? What were you doing? What did you have? Did anything change in your life over the past ten years? Time seems to stand still when you look at a clock waiting for the next hour to come. It may seem like nothing is happening in your life right now. You go to work, day in and day out, making just enough money to keep from calling yourself homeless. Or you are out of work, figuratively knocking on every door you can think of for a job. At the end of the day, you collapse in bed, looking at the same news that you heard yesterday, or last week, or last month. If your science teacher hadn't told you, you might have thought that the earth stood still, while the sun revolved about it.

Waiting as described in the above passage does not mean that you life is on hold. It means that the Lord is doing His thing, because, quite frankly, all the pieces that come together in your life to keep you safe and moving forward are not under your control. Watch a little child waiting to grab something, like a wrapped piece of food. The parent may politely and gently say, "Wait a minute, while I unwrap this." The child reluctantly waits for the parent to unwrap the food item, and present it in a safe and consumable fashion.

Can you wait for the Lord to do His thing? God truly works miracles in your life, while you are waiting, because, the world never stops turning, even when you are asleep. It's been said that children grow when they are sleeping. And when you wake up, refreshed and energized, looking at a new day with new possibilities, God has prepared the path for you, so that you can go out into this world with renewed strength and energy.

HAVE NO FEAR. GOD IS HERE!

When my father and my mother forsake me, then the LORD will take me up.

Teach me thy way, O LORD, and lead me in a plain path, because of mine enemies.

Deliver me not over unto the will of mine enemies: for false witnesses are risen up against me, and such as breathe out cruelty.

I had fainted, unless I had believed to see the goodness of the LORD in the land of the living.

Wait on the LORD: be of good courage, and he shall strengthen thine heart: wait, I say, on the LORD.

Psalm 27:10-14

When I haven't done anything wrong (at least in my mind), and someone has shown evil hatred toward me, I go to this passage. We all have been victims of false accusations, some minor, some major. It can be a really hurting feeling. Maybe we didn't get a chance to "defend" ourselves, our pride, and our hurting hearts, for any of many reasons. You go to work and sit down to type up a report and in comes the boss fussing with you about something that was not your fault, or something that didn't happen, or something that someone misinterpreted your actions and were highly offended. You want to fight back, and of course there is a time when that is appropriate. But sometimes, you just have to turn the other cheek and let God handle it.

Bullying and social media mayhem, in which you do not know who your false accuser is, can make it harder to confront the "invisible enemy." Have no fear, whatever man may say about you, because God is here to fight your battles, even the invisible enemy. He knows your heart. He knows the truth. This may sound strange, but in many cases, so does your enemy, because God has a way of communicating to them in the spirit. Let God comfort you, when no one else will. When you stand innocently accused of something, remember to be of good courage, because God is here to strengthen you.

SOMETHING TO SING ABOUT!

*O sing unto the LORD a new song; for he hath
done marvellous things: his right hand, and his
holy arm, hath gotten him the victory.*

*The LORD hath made known his salvation: his
righteousness hath he openly shewed in the sight
of the heathen.*

*He hath remembered his mercy and his truth
toward the house of Israel: all the ends of the earth
have seen the salvation of our God.*

*Make a joyful noise unto the LORD, all the earth:
make a loud noise, and rejoice, and sing praise.*

*Sing unto the LORD with the harp; with the
harp, and the voice of a psalm.*

Psalm 98:1-5

There is a lot of singing in churches. Sometimes people get so happy that they clap their hands, stomp their feet to the beat, and shout. What is all the fuss about? The Lord offers us salvation. The Lord has shown us mercy. Ever watch some TV game shows where the winner wins a few hundred dollars or prizes and jumps up and down with joy? Compare the eternal salvation that God offers us to the short-lived material things, and we all should be shouting and singing, even when we have not won a material prize. One thing I like about being a Christian is that we are all winners.

Don't wait for Sunday morning service to sing, "Praise the Lord. Halleluiah! Thank You, Jesus!" Don't wait for the radio gospel channel to come on. Don't wait for your favorite TV preacher to come on. Sing to your heart's delight, because you have something to sing about!

TURN ON THE LIGHT, PLEASE

Jesus cried and said, He that believeth on me, believeth not on me, but on him that sent me.

And he that seeth me seeth him that sent me.

I am come a light into the world, that whosoever believeth on me should not abide in darkness.

John 12:44-46

Safety is first when going down stairs. Hold on to the railing. Watch your step. Don't block your view with a large package or laundry basket. Pay attention to when the steps start and end. Avoid slippers that could slip off of you while going up and down the stairs. Also, just as important is to not walk down stairs in the dark. I don't want to guess at how many people do that.

Jesus knows people try to go through life in the dark, not knowing where their next step will land. It is so comforting to read about His analogy of being the light to the world. He can guide us and show us the way to go ahead of time. The Holy Spirit is that light. There are spiritual pitfalls that He can warn us about to avoid. It is like having an internal flashlight that points us in the right direction. Of course, it is up to us to "turn on the light" so that we don't trip in the darkness of sin. I am asking you politely, for your own safety to please turn on Jesus' light and see your blessings.

HE FOUND YOU

*For the Son of man is come to seek and to save
that which was lost.*

Luke 19:10

Imagine that you are driving down a familiar road in your home town. Imagine that you have traveled that way for at least ten years. You estimate how long it will take you from point A to point B. It is almost dinner time and you are looking forward to sitting down after a long day at work or school and just chilling out to look at your favorite TV program. Then you look ahead for the familiar corner traffic lights, which are blinking, instead of a solid red or green. The traffic officer redirects you to a detour, down a road you are not familiar with. You watch carefully to see which way the detour will lead you to get back on the street that gets you home. Only this time, the detour is not clear. Now what? You are lost, and you know it. But actually, you were lost the minute you got in your car to travel the route that was no longer available to you. You just didn't know it when you set out to go home.

Life can be like that. We are often lost and do not know it. We think someone in our life will always be with us. We think we will have that job until we are ready to retire. We think that we understood someone when we made a commitment to them. We think we can resist the Devil's temptations of greed and envy. We go down one road, but get sidetracked to a detour. The miracle of God's gifts to us is that He finds us even when we didn't know we were lost. If you know you are lost, He finds you too. No matter how lost and forgotten you may feel, wherever you are, He will find you. And when he finds you, say, "Thanks for the directions, Lord."

41

A PROMISE IS A PROMISE

The Lord is not slack concerning his promise, as some men count slackness; but is longsuffering to us-ward, not willing that any should perish, but that all should come to repentance.

II Peter 3:9

There are some people, as long as they are breathing, when they say they will do something, they will do it. Then there are others, well, we won't get into that. Let's just say, when some people offer you a Plan A, you need to have a Plan B, just in case. People often have good intentions. They get overcommitted. They forget. Or they may even be "shy" about getting out of things so they just say they were going to do something for you, with no intention of doing it. They may have said, "I can't do that now, because you didn't do what you promised to do." Excuses often come with failed promises.

Then there are the promises we give to others. Of course, that is different. We meant well, but something got in the way. It is all part of life, trying to be good, when we all fall short in one way or another.

Have you ever built your hopes up hoping that someone would come through on their promise, only to be greatly disappointed when they renege in it? Well, God is not like that. What He says He will do, He will do. He might have to wait for us to come to Him and trust Him, after all the bad disappointments that people have been to you. He knows that you have had some bad experiences from people making empty promises. Rest assured, He will keep His promise.

BE AN EXAMPLE

Ask, and it shall be given you; seek, and ye shall find; knock, and it shall be opened unto you:

For every one that asketh receiveth; and he that seeketh findeth; and to him that knocketh it shall be opened.

Or what man is there of you, whom if his son ask bread, will he give him a stone?

Or if he ask a fish, will he give him a serpent?

If ye then, being evil, know how to give good gifts unto your children, how much more shall your Father which is in heaven give good things to them that ask him?

Therefore all things whatsoever ye would that men should do to you, do ye even so to them: for this is the law and the prophets.

Matthew 7:7-12

Christ throughout His ministry on earth was an example for us to follow as Christians. He represented love, kindness, compassion and patience, because He knew that is what we wanted from others. If someone comes to you in need, look to Christ's behavior on what to do. I know we are not perfect and will fall short of His perfect example, but that doesn't mean that we should stop trying to be like Him.

Put yourself in their shoes. How would you like to be treated? Ask yourself that question when someone in your life has "messed up" or "doesn't come up to your standards." Are you forgiving, understanding, and loving? Be an example for others to follow you, as you have followed Christ.

STAYING IN TODAY

Wherefore, if God so clothe the grass of the field, which to day is, and to morrow is cast into the oven, shall he not much more clothe you, O ye of little faith? Therefore take no thought, saying, What shall we eat? or, What shall we drink? or, Wherewithal shall we be clothed? (For after all these things do the Gentiles seek:) for your heavenly Father knoweth that ye have need of all these things. But seek ye first the kingdom of God, and his righteousness; and all these things shall be added unto you. Take therefore no thought for the morrow: for the morrow shall take thought for the things of itself. Sufficient unto the day is the evil thereof.

Matthew 6:30-34

Worry can cause us to mess up big time in our relationships with others. Yeah, they didn't do what they were supposed to do. It's done. The past cannot be undone. We worry about our own conduct too. We know we have this bad habit that is so hard to kick. Then there are the external things like the weather and the economy. Will we have a job tomorrow? Will we have a house next week?

There is someone who can be of great help in these situations. He knows all of the things that can go right and wrong. He knows everything about you and the other person and the earth's changing environment. We have to deal with where we are in our life. We just can't completely sort out all of the variables in life ahead of time, like storms, the economy, life and death.

If we tried to figure out every bad thing that could happen or might happen, our brains could be overloaded, and in some cases, result in acute anxiety attacks. Not a pretty picture. Take comfort in knowing that God's got this thing called life. Keep your mind focused on staying in today.

LIGHTEN UP

Come unto me, all ye that labour and are heavy laden, and I will give you rest.

Take my yoke upon you, and learn of me; for I am meek and lowly in heart: and ye shall find rest unto your souls.

For my yoke is easy, and my burden is light.

Matthew 11:28-30

When you get it "right" you will feel a heavy load off of your shoulder. Sometimes it is as distinct as feeling the presence of the Holy Spirit or angel coming into your room and lifting the emotional weight off of you, giving you renewed faith and gratitude. You will know that God instructs us on things that at first may seem like a burden to us, but in the whole scheme of things, He gives us relief from our burdens. Guilt, regrets, missed this and that, must do this and that, He has the answer to them all. That answer includes, "I love you. I will protect you. I want the best thing for you."

Take a deep breath. Blow it out slowly. Think about God's love for you. Think about how He brought you out of some difficult situations in the past. These might have been things that only He could have done.

The more you read and study the Bible and learn about God, you will see that He has already lightened your burden, and there is no reason for Him to stop now.

BELIEVE IT TO ACHIEVE IT

*Jesus answered and said unto them, Verily I say unto
you, If ye have faith, and doubt not, ye shall not
only do this which is done to the fig tree, but also if
ye shall say unto this mountain, Be thou removed,
and be thou cast into the sea; it shall be done.*

*And all things, whatsoever ye shall ask in prayer,
believing, ye shall receive.*

Matthew 21:21-22

People have overcome great odds, by not giving up too
soon. Ask Thomas Edison about that. When you really believe
something, your behavior will act accordingly. This can make
the difference between success and failure. Jesus knew that if
people did not believe in Him, they would not act as Christians.
Then they would wonder why they could not do this or that.

There is some scientific support for achieving believable
goals. You greatly increase your likelihood of achieving a goal if
you actually believe it is achievable. So don't sell yourself short.
Believer it to achieve it.

CLUTCHING FOR A CURE

*And, behold, a woman, which was diseased with
an issue of blood twelve years, came behind him,
and touched the hem of his garment:*

*For she said within herself, If I may but touch his
garment, I shall be whole.*

*But Jesus turned him about, and when he saw
her, he said, Daughter, be of good comfort; thy
faith hath made thee whole. And the woman was
made whole from that hour.*

Matthew 9:20-22

Ever wanted something so bad that you could see it and touch it, even though it may not be anywhere in physical sight? To the outside world, one might ask regarding the woman with the issue of blood for twelve years, "Why didn't she just give up?" But we do not know what the Holy Spirit was telling her. It may have told her, "This is the day," or, "Just reach out and touch His garment." Why else would she risk going out in public with the stigma attached to women in those days?

She knew, that she knew, that she knew. She knew Christ was a healer. She knew He could heal her if He saw her. She knew if she just reached out and did her part, He would do His.

It takes determination to overcome great odds. A person who is not popular, didn't grow up on the rich side of town, or had societal setbacks, often knows about struggling to survive. It is not how long the race is but how determined one is to continue running toward the prize.

It doesn't matter if no one else sees your vision but you. It doesn't matter if you have no idea how you are going to get from point "A" to point "B." It doesn't matter how long it takes. Man makes the choice, but God makes the timing.

Twelve years, five years, or one year is a long time to wait for something. What did the woman do during those twelve years? We don't know, but I doubt if she spent it feeling sorry for herself, or complaining to everyone within an earshot of her, of how miserable she was. She had to have an optimistic viewpoint, a strong will that her troubles wouldn't last forever. In general, if you lay around feeling sorry for yourself long enough, you will find it harder to get up out of bed. That is not a good thing.

Plants take a season to push themselves out of the dark dirt, up toward the sun and cleansing rain, before they blossom to full beauty. Who told the plants to do this? God's infinite wisdom has us covered over until the right time and place. So keep reaching for your reward. Help others while waiting. Your turn will come too.

CHRIST'S CORNER

*For they all saw him, and were troubled. And
immediately he talked with them, and saith unto
them, Be of good cheer: it is I; be not afraid.*

Mark 6:50

Scary news and events happen, most of which we can't do
anything about. It takes a lot of faith to tune it out and be
cheerful on top of that. How can we be cheerful in a world of
disease, violence, poverty and natural disasters? I don't think
you can without the Lord's help. If Christ said to be of good
cheer and not afraid, there must be a way to do that.

That way includes the guidance and comfort of the Holy
Spirit. We can learn to trust Him to bring us through difficult
times. Yes, the waves get rough. But the good news is that the
grave is not our final resting place. I have started with that as
the worst that could happen to a person. There are far lesser
things that we face daily that can get us fearful, like applying
for a job, or meeting a new person, or taking a test. Most of the
time, the fear is much greater than the reality.

If you can be cheerful, that is a major blessing. If you can't
do anything about a situation, then why worry about it? We are
all human and have our weaknesses. Just be aware of your full
options. You can smile in the middle of a storm. You can laugh
at a loss possession. You can rejoice among ruins. It is possible
and, if you can find your way to do that, don't be afraid of life.
Don't miss your blessings because you were brooding. Don't
hide from a hill that seems too high to climb. Because, one thing
is for sure, whatever you are going through, Christ is right
there with you to carry you through it, if necessary. He is just
around the corner waiting for you. Come to Christ's corner for
comfort.

IT'S POSSIBLE

And they were astonished out of measure, saying among themselves, Who then can be saved?

And Jesus looking upon them saith, With men it is impossible, but not with God: for with God all things are possible.

Mark 10:26-27

They said it was impossible to fly. They said it was impossible to reach the moon. They even said man can't run a mile under 4 minutes. If I had a dollar for everything man said was impossible, I would be at least a multi-millionaire. Who is to say what is possible and what isn't?

When you read the thousands of laws that the Old Testament listed, it does seem impossible to be saved. But that is not how Christ saw it. God found a way to say yes.

He gave His Son as a living sacrifice to save us from our sins. What seemed impossible became possible.

When you have a vision and dream to fulfill a purpose, ask the Lord to guide you step-by-step. The first step is to believe "It's possible."

IS IT WORTH IT?

So when this corruptible shall have put on incorruption,
and this mortal shall have put on immortality, then
shall be brought to pass the saying that is written,
Death is swallowed up in victory. O death, where is
thy sting? O grave, where is thy victory? The sting of
death is sin; and the strength of sin is the law.

But thanks be to God, which giveth us the victory
through our Lord Jesus Christ. Therefore, my beloved
brethren, be ye stedfast, unmoveable, always abounding
in the work of the Lord, forasmuch as ye know that your
labour is not in vain in the Lord.

I Corinthians 15:54-58

At some point in this journey called "life" you will have to make some difficult decisions. For those decisions where the risks are low, it is not a big deal if you make them, like which sock to wear in the morning. Then there are major decisions. You know in your heart that this decision will affect the rest of your life. Many times you will get an uneasy feeling inside of you as the Holy Spirit is urging you to do or not do something. You look at what you know and you don't understand why the Holy Spirit is telling you these things. It doesn't make sense to you at that time and moment. However, you may have had that uneasy feeling before and as time went by, the less obvious became obvious.

In the passage above, Paul is saying when you do the right thing you will have victory over death through eternal salvation granted to you by our Lord Jesus Christ. Is it worth it to stand up to your convictions? Is it worth it to be a Christian? Is it worth it to do what is right, even under pressure to do otherwise? If you have confessed your sins and believe Christ is your Savior, the answer is, "Yes." It is worth it because you are worth it.

INCREASE WHEN YOU INCREASE

*And the apostles said unto the Lord, Increase our
faith. And the Lord said, If ye had faith as a grain of
mustard seed, ye might say unto this sycamine tree,
Be thou plucked up by the root, and be thou planted
in the sea; and it should obey you.*

Luke 17:5, 6

It has happened over and over again. People who don't give up on their dreams and goals often reach them, no matter how far fetched they may seem to others. No one has your vision but you. No one has your purpose in life but you. Didn't go to college, but want to teach at a college? It's possible. Can't sing, but want to be a top billboard singer? It's possible. Don't have feet and missing parts of both of your legs but want to run track in Olympic competition? It's possible.

All Christians start out with some faith, like babes. As we mature we should be increasing in faith. As a "child" listening to your pastor preach about faith, it may not make a lot of sense to you. However, over time, your faith can get stronger and stronger. You start believing that you could do things that you didn't think you could do before. You started paying more attention to the Holy Spirit and studying the Holy Bible more. When you increase your faith, you increase your blessings.

WHICH WAY DO I TURN?

*Let not your heart be troubled: ye believe in God, believe
also in me. In my Father's house are many mansions:
if it were not so, I would have told you. I go to prepare
a place for you.*

*And if I go and prepare a place for you, I will come
again, and receive you unto myself; that where I am,
there ye may be also. And whither I go ye know, and
the way ye know.*

*Thomas saith unto him, Lord, we know not whither
thou goest; and how can we know the way?*

*Jesus saith unto him, I am the way, the truth, and the
life: no man cometh unto the Father, but by me. If ye
had known me, ye should have known my Father also:
and from henceforth ye know him, and have seen him.*

John 14:1-7

You are on a treasure hunt and you are walking around in a
maze trying to find the hidden treasure. Someone said it was in
a mansion, but you don't see any mansion in sight. Looking for
the Kingdom of God can be like that. You know something
good is waiting for you but which way do you turn?

If there is one major sub-theme throughout the Bible, it is
the seemingly unpredictable twists and turns of living. It can be
very stressful not knowing what is going to happen tomorrow.
You plan your life and your day one way and it turns out
another way. Jesus is telling us in the above scripture that in the
end, everything is going to be alright. Just relax and stop
worrying so much.

When you feel lost, turn to Jesus. When you feel depressed,
turn to Jesus. He will guide you to His Father's house where
you will find peace, love and joy. So when you don't know
which way to turn, turn to Jesus.

IN JESUS' NAME WE PRAY

Verily, verily, I say unto you, He that believeth on me, the works that I do shall he do also; and greater works than these shall he do; because I go unto my Father.

And whatsoever ye shall ask in my name, that will I do, that the Father may be glorified in the Son.

If ye shall ask any thing in my name, I will do it.

John 14:12-14

God is a God of divine order. Miraculous things can happen to people that support God's divine order. It may not seem like God is answering your prayer, but if you pray in Jesus' name for God's divine will to be fulfilled by your actions, you can do great works.

He knows what is best for us, even when we don't know ourselves. Would you ask God for a sinful thing? Of course you would not. Asking for a blessing in Jesus' name is an essential part of God's promise to answer your requests.

Believing in Jesus is also an essential part of your requests. God is not to be treated like a genie that you make a frivolous wish and out pops the event or item. That is not what God is about. He is about love, peace and forgiveness. Pray for those things and you will find a more than willing God to answer your prayers.

DID YOU OPEN YOUR GIFT?

But the Comforter, which is the Holy Ghost, whom the Father will send in my name, he shall teach you all things, and bring all things to your remembrance, whatsoever I have said unto you. Peace I leave with you, my peace I give unto you: not as the world giveth, give I unto you. Let not your heart be troubled, neither let it be afraid.

John 14:26, 27

The Holy Ghost was sent by God to comfort us and give us peace of mind. We did not have to buy it. It was already paid for by the sacrifice of Jesus Christ. There are different definitions of peace. This one represents peace of mind. When you are worrying about something, reach back to this scripture and remember that the Comforter is there to not only guide you through the storms of life, but also to give you peace.

This gift to be fully operative must be opened and received by you. What a wonderful present. Listen to the Comforter who can tell you things about your desires, dreams and disappointments that no other source could reveal. When tragedy hits, it is only human to question why it happened to you. Many times the people around us just can't explain why it happened. Your body and mind may be wrenching in emotional and even physical pain.

The good news is that you have a choice to stay in resentment, anger, unforgiveness, withdrawal, and depression or make the choice of compassion, love, contentment, forgiveness and peace. Some people take weeks, months and years in misery. They may have tried everything thing but peace of mind, including alcohol and drugs that do not cure the pain. Then one day, the Comforter communicates to them in a unique way that finally helps them to let go. It may be a bird on a fence, or a small whisper in the dark, or a special passage in the Bible. Whatever it is, you may get the sense that you are not alone, that the Holy Spirit is letting you know that you are going to be alright, no matter what. How long will it take you to open your gift? Do it now.

TURNING OLD TO NEW

(For we walk by faith, not by sight:)

Therefore if any man be in Christ, he is a new creature: old things are passed away; behold, all things are become new.

For he hath made him to be sin for us, who knew no sin; that we might be made the righteousness of God in him.

II Corinthians 5:7, 17, 21

In the natural progression of people and things, when they are first born or created, they are new. As time progresses, the new gets old, and if a living thing, deteriorates considerably over time. However, that is not the case in the spiritual life of a human being. We come into this world as sinners, but through faith we become new creatures of righteousness.

Think about how unusual that sounds, i.e. that the old becomes new. What a miracle that is. I welcome the opportunity for a fresh start. Every day is a new day to be a new person. With faith you can grow from old to new. You messed up in life. Start over. You procrastinated for years on fulfilling your purpose. Start over. You said some bad things to someone. Start over. You broke the law. Start over. No other law or policy or procedure can make or reverse something from totally old to totally new. By definition, if it is old, it is not new. But God can make all things new. Just take a moment right now to think just how amazing that is. Now say, "Hello. Good to meet me."

WHO'S YOUR CHEERLEADER?

I rejoice therefore that I have confidence in you in all things.

II Corinthians 7:16

Ever given an assignment or task that you have never done before? It can be scary. There is nothing like someone having confidence in your ability to do your assignment well. Parents encourage their children to do well by assuring them that they can do a certain thing. While watching a young child reading a children's book, notice that a few of the words may be difficult to read. The overseeing parent helps out by saying things like, "Good job. You can do it. Just sound it out. Whoa! What a good reader you are." The child may fidget around, but keeping his eyes on the word, and his ears on those encouraging words, he manages to speak it correctly.

As we become adults, we may get fewer of those, "You can do it." Sometimes we want feedback so badly that we ask the loving person next to us, "How did I do?" How much nicer if we got that unsolicited. If no one else will, God will encourage you. He will be your biggest fan when you do right. When things get overwhelming and you don't know how you are going to get "everything" or "anything" done, turn to God. He can tell you which foot to put in front of the other. He can put your life in order. He has confidence in you, because He wouldn't give you a task that you couldn't handle.

Now if you are doing too much and are too busy, He will tell you that too. He wants you to focus on the important things that will make your life and the people around you better. So be encouraged and keep trying to achieve your goals, because God is your biggest cheerleader.

AN EVEN PLAYING FIELD

Then Peter opened his mouth, and said, Of a truth I perceive that God is no respecter of persons:

But in every nation he that feareth him, and worketh righteousness, is accepted with him.

Acts 10:34, 35

"No respecter of persons" has a very special meaning to "minority" groups. Sometimes you are given different rules to play on the field of housing, mortgages, jobs, and education. In many places in the world, which family you were born into determines your social and economic destiny, regardless of your abilities. However, no one is a "minority" in God's eyes. Everyone who confesses their sins and claims Jesus as their Savior is respected and welcomed into the family of Christians.

Believers are accepted by God. It doesn't matter if you are black, white, yellow, brown or red. It doesn't matter if you are rich or poor. It doesn't matter if you are free or in prison. You have the exact same rights and privileges as the next person, regardless of you socio-economic status. What a blessing that is. Thank you, Lord! I receive that. Let the games of life begin!

SOMEONE IS WAITING FOR YOU

Beloved, now are we the sons of God, and it doth
not yet appear what we shall be: but we know
that, when he shall appear, we shall be like him;
for we shall see him as he is.

And every man that hath this hope in him
purifieth himself, even as he is pure.

I John 3:2, 3

Take just a moment to take yourself away from the day-to-day to-do lists of living. Imagine that you are in heaven walking around and seeing God. It is hard to imagine as human beings exactly what God would look like. Will He be in a long white flowing robe? Will He shine like the sun or bright light? Will Jesus be sitting next to Him at a table full of food?

I don't know. But I do know He will be there in heaven and the pure shall see Him. It really is a mystery that man has been trying to figure out for centuries. Some people have claimed to have been to heaven and returned. I think the most important thing about the above passage is that He will be waiting for us. Will you be there?

CHEER UP

These things I have spoken unto you, that in me ye might have peace. In the world ye shall have tribulation: but be of good cheer; I have overcome the world.

John 16:33

Like storms, most personal troubles come and go. Everyone has to deal with the unpleasant things of life. However, after a good rain (and to farmers, rain that is not excessive is a good rain), sometimes you see a rainbow. It is amazing how people like rainbows. They are pretty, but there is more than their looks that gives us comfort. They signify the end of a storm. They lift and connect your eyes to the sky and back down to the earth. They can remind us of God's powerful hand over the universe. Of course there is now a scientific basis for the existence of a rainbow, but that is not what lifts your spirit. It is the visible evidence of something greater.

When problems come your way, remember that there is a power greater than the problem. Remember that we humans of every color are like rainbows that God has created to connect our souls between heaven and earth. So cheer up pretty rainbow. Your creator has already overcome the world's ills. And even though you may not currently see a rainbow, it's there in you, waiting for the Son to shine and brighten the world through you, again.

CHRISTIANS BELIEVE IN CHRIST

And every spirit that confesseth not that Jesus Christ is come in the flesh is not of God: and this is that spirit of antichrist, whereof ye have heard that it should come; and even now already is it in the world.

Ye are of God, little children, and have overcome them: because greater is he that is in you, than he that is in the world.

I John 4:3-4

Our God is a forgiving God. Our God is patient. Our God is loving and compassionate. But one thing our God is not: a liar. Sometimes people quote the Holy Scripture passages that are convenient for their point of view. Then they "qualify it" by saying things like Christ did not come in the flesh as a human, died, rose from the dead and ascended into heaven. Do you believe that He was born of the Virgin Mary and died to cleanse us of our sins so that we may have eternal salvation? Well, if you are a Christian that is exactly what you believe.

There is no power greater than God, the one and only God. Christians also believe that there are evil forces who attempt to confuse you by pretending to be more powerful than God. They will lie to you, steal, and most dangerously, lull you into confusion. What better way to separate you from believing in Christ than to say He was not God. If they say that Christ did not come into this world in the flesh, they are not representing Christians.

If you want to be a Christian then you must believe in Christ. Amen.

HOPE, JOY, AND PEACE. WHOA!

Now the God of hope fill you with all joy and
peace in believing, that ye may abound in hope,
through the power of the Holy Ghost.

Roman 15:13

Ever watch one of those info-commercials. They demonstrate a gadget that will do amazing things like chop, peal and slice, all from one easy-to-use appliance. Then after you get excited about it, they give you the low discounted, limited-time price that you can't get anywhere else. But that's not all. They throw in an optional attachment that can do even more things, that is absolutely "free." But that's not all. They double or triple the quantity, so that you get two or three of them for the same low price of one. You may go, "What a bargain! Whoa! I want that."

A lot is packed into the above Bible scripture. You get lots of hope. Hope is what helps a person persevere through challenging experiences. With hope you can get out of bed, looking toward a better day than the one you had yesterday. With hope you can continue to pursue your goals and dreams, in spite of others who might discourage you. With hope you can see your loved ones again that have gone on before you. With hope you can bring new beings into the world, as God intended to multiply the earth, hoping that they will have a better world than today's.

And that's not all. You get joy. With joy, you can smile. With joy you can be a witness of Christ's goodness to others. With joy, you can have the rewards of life. With joy you can say, "Praise the Lord!"

And that's not all. You also get peace. With peace of mind, you can reduce the stress in your life. With peace, you can stay calm while everyone around you is freaking out. With peace, you can forgive and love your enemies, because you know that is one way to break the cycle of violence.

And that's not all. God fills you up with hope, joy and peace, so that you will have a lifetime supply and never run out.

But the best part of God's offer is that it is free! Christ paid for all of it. Now, that's a good deal. Whoa!

WHAT YOU DON'T SEE, YOU GET.

But as it is written, Eye hath not seen, nor ear heard, neither have entered into the heart of man, the things which God hath prepared for them that love him. But God hath revealed them unto us by his Spirit: for the Spirit searcheth all things, yea, the deep things of God.

I Corinthians 2:9, 10

Some people like surprises. Some people do not. There are surprise birthday parties. There are surprise gifts. There are even surprise greeting cards. There are surprise phone calls. There are surprise pregnancies. A parent may buy Christmas presents for their children and hide them. The little child tries to find them; and even imagines in great anticipation what she will get. But it isn't until the parent reveals and presents the gift to the child on Christmas Day that the child fully sees it.

God knows that it is hard for us to imagine all of the wonderful things He has in store for us. We may try to peek and see what is next around the corner of our curiosity. He knows all about human nature. He also knows that some of us want at least some kind of hint about heaven and our future blessings. So He sent us the Holy Spirit to reveal *some* things to us. Not everything, but enough for us to handle in whatever season is in our lives.

He does tell us, that what He has prepared for us, we have never seen before. That means it will be somewhat of a surprise. I am amazed at some of the things God reveals to me through the Holy Spirit. There may have been no other way to know them. Then there are things I don't understand and seek the answers to that elude me. Take comfort that God knows just how much you need to know and when you need to know it. But, whatever your blessings are, they will be "out of sight." Just because you don't "see" it doesn't mean you won't get it.

MEET YOUR SPOKESPERSON

For we are saved by hope: but hope that is seen is not hope: for what a man seeth, why doth he yet hope for?

But if we hope for that we see not, then do we with patience wait for it.

Likewise the Spirit also helpeth our infirmities: for we know not what we should pray for as we ought: but the Spirit itself maketh intercession for us with groanings which cannot be uttered.

Romans 8: 24-26

Wouldn't it be nice to have your own personal spokesperson sometimes? Some people have the gift of gab. They know exactly what they want and how to say it. But do they always? From time to time, even the most talkative person is speechless, or should have been. I don't think there is a person alive who didn't have regrets about something they said or failed to say.

Because so many things are out of our control, we have to learn to let go and let God handle some things. We may have no idea how to solve a problem or get out of a fix. We may be comfortable with our choices, but see others who are lost in life. So we also pray for them. What a blessing to know that if we skip just one critical element in our petitions (prayers) to God, the Holy Spirit can intercede and fill in the missing pieces of our prayer.

That way, nothing is left out of what we are asking God to do. So if you have not met your spokesperson, the Holy Spirit, let me introduce you. The Holy Spirit is part of the Holy Trinity, which is the Father, Son, and Holy Spirit. They are three in one. So you know your message will get to God. There is no doubt about it. You couldn't ask for a better spokesperson on your behalf.

A GOOD REPORT CARD

Now faith is the substance of things hoped for, the evidence of things not seen.

For by it the elders obtained a good report. Through faith we understand that the worlds were framed by the word of God, so that things which are seen were not made of things which do appear.

Hebrews 11:1-3

This is a very familiar passage to many Christians, about faith being the evidence of things not seen. Less familiar may be the verses that immediately follow it, which can bring tremendous comfort when dealing with the "unseen" issues of life. Knowing that through faith you will get a good report can help allay some of your fears. For example, you don't know if you will get that job, or promotion, but if God reveals it to you, through faith, you know that you will hear some good news.

Of course, not everything that happens to you will feel like a good report. The point is that it is important to be in tuned with your faith so that what may not be obvious to you now doesn't mean that bad things will happen in a particular situation. You may get a warning that the day will have some challenges and, through your faith, you prepare yourself as best you can. But no matter what happens to you on that day, or any other day, you know through faith that God is in control of the world. Stay faithful to God and He will stay faithful to you. The interim report card may not look so good from time to time, but your final report card markings will be good. God is good at "changing grades."

CAN YOU SEE GOOD?

Nevertheless he left not himself without witness,
in that he did good, and gave us rain from
heaven, and fruitful seasons, filling our hearts
with food and gladness.

Acts 14:17

This is such an upbeat passage that I love reading it over and over. I like it a lot. It's a good message. My goodness! When you want to focus on the good things, turn to this passage. After the rain from heaven, comes fruitful seasons. This passage is just dripping with goodness. Are you feeling down about something right now? Take a moment to meditate on this scripture. It didn't say that you will never experience cloudy days or bad things. It didn't say that all you have to do is snap your fingers and instantly sunshine and harvest would appear. It takes time to grow a good harvest. You take time to become a mature Christian.

But, for now, imagine seeing good things happening in your life. Imagine you have a great relationship. Imagine you have more money in the bank. See yourself getting better in health. See that dream career in your life. Can you see good things in your life? Can you see all the healthy food you want and should eat, resulting in a slimmer, healthier you? What a view! Goodness, gracious!

BOXES OF PEACE

Therefore being justified by faith, we have peace with God through our Lord Jesus Christ:

By whom also we have access by faith into this grace wherein we stand, and rejoice in hope of the glory of God.

Romans 5:1, 2

It has been said, "The best things in life are free." When it comes to peace of mind, that is true, as far as what we personally pay to get it. So why don't more people get peace? Maybe it is because they do not open their gift boxes. If only it were something visibly tangible, maybe more people would accept God's gift of peace.

I wish I could wrap it up in a box, give it to Santa Claus and request that he delivers it to everybody's homes in the world. I wish that when that box arrives down the chimney, and rolls over to a place under your Christmas tree, that the package would be so bright and pretty that you excitedly open that box with great anticipation.

I wish that when you open your gift of peace that you take it out of the box and wear it immediately. When your family sees that you are wearing peace all over your face, I wish that they will look in their boxes and get their peace too.

Then finally, I wish that you call Jesus up on your spiritual phone and thank Him for your present of peace by saying, "It's the best gift I have ever had. It's perfect!" You make peace real when you open your box of peace and wear it. Merry Christmas!

WHICH COMES FIRST, PROMISE OR PATIENCE?

Cast not away therefore your confidence, which hath great recompence of reward.

For ye have need of patience, that, after ye have done the will of God, ye might receive the promise.

Hebrews 10:35, 36

Athletics know patience is the key to winning. They have to practice with confidence that eventually they will win the game. Seamstresses delicately catch up just one strand in a fabric as they patiently hem a garment. Students must diligently listen to the teacher, do their homework, and prepare for the examination, in order to get a good grade. Writers must have patience, as they type one letter at a time on their computer way before selling a bestseller. Most great accomplishments are preceded by great patience.

Yet, sometimes we pray with our eyes closed and when we are done and open them, we look around for God's immediate fulfillment of that petition. It doesn't always work that way. We have to have patience and confidence in God's perfect timing. He will fulfill His promise. It is not easy to wait for God's actions. But with practice, over time, you will receive your rewards on earth and in heaven.

David, who had been anointed king long before he actually ruled Israel had an impatient moment when he was on the run from King Saul's wrath. He and his roaming army were hungry. When a rich man named Nabal refused to offer him food, David got very angry and was about to kill all of the man's family. However, God sent the rich man's wife, Abigail, who brought peace offerings of food. She also warned David not to blow receiving God's promise to him that he would be king. Fortunately for David, he listened to her and did eventually

71

become king (I Samuel 25).

Take a deep breath through the nose. Let it out slowly. Count to ten, backwards. Go for a walk. Do whatever works for you to develop patience, because patience in deed, precedes receiving the promise.

HE UNDERSTANDS

Rejoice in the Lord always: and again I say, Rejoice. Let your moderation be known unto all men. The Lord is at hand. Be careful for nothing; but in every thing by prayer and supplication with thanksgiving let your requests be made known unto God. And the peace of God, which passeth all understanding, shall keep your hearts and minds through Christ Jesus.

Philippians 4: 4-7

Have you tried to explain something to someone and they just didn't get it? God is not like that. He understands what you want, need, and don't need. He is like an interpreter on your behalf. Life is too short and complicated to try to understand and learn everything there is to know in the world. Search your heart and communicate in love the best way you can. Be happy about the Lord being in your life. Do the best that you can.

Nobody is perfect. Pray to God about how to handle a task that seems too difficult. Just because you do not know how to do something at a given point in time, doesn't mean that God won't give you the best way to do it. We already know that God's way is the best way. So that is a good reason to rejoice before we know the outcome. Let Jesus walk you through your assignments. But first you need to pray for His hand of guidance and wisdom.

Then there are people in your life that you just don't understand. Why do they behave this way or that? Perhaps a psychiatrist could explain it better to you. But how many people are mental health professionals that you can just call up and ask? Of course, they may not know either. Maybe the person is having a physical condition that you can't figure out. You may not have access to their medical records. You may not understand your own mental and physical condition. God does, so you don't have to. He knows your language and the rest of the world's language too. He needs no interpreter.

ONE DAY AT-A-TIME CONTENTMENT

Not that I speak in respect of want: for I have learned,
in whatsoever state I am, therewith to be content.

Philippians 4:11

From the day we are born, we have wants and desires, starting with wanting to be warm and not cold. As we get older our want list gets longer. Is it a new house, or car? Whatever it is, it is usually less than what we have.

Most people, no matter how much they have or how rich they are, want more of something. I don't think of contentment as never to dream or wish or get goals. I think of contentment as trying to do the best I can each day. When the day is over, being content to rest in the Lord's arm of grace gives me comfort. It is forgiving myself and others for the imperfections of life. It is stopping to say, "I am alright and at peace with myself." It is truly a state of mind that can help you get needed rest so you can start all over again the next day renewed and refreshed.

Being content helps you to let go of anger and grudges, self-hate and projected hatreds. Look at the world news and you know that things are not like you want them to be, because so many other people are not content. Let God comfort you and give you peace of mind in your day's contentment.

UNITED IN VICTORY

*Nay, in all these things we are more than
conquerors through him that loved us.*

*For I am persuaded, that neither death, nor life,
nor angels, nor principalities, nor powers, nor
things present, nor things to come,*

*Nor height, nor depth, nor any other creature,
shall be able to separate us from the love of God,
which is in Christ Jesus our Lord.*

Romans 8:37-39

One of the best things about being a Christian is that we can all be winners. We can help others to be victorious without diminishing in any way our winnings. There are evil spiritual forces using people to do evil things. So we do have enemies. Yet, when we unite as Christians with love, we can conquer even death.

Christ's love unites us with Him. We gain our strength to succeed through love. Don't try to fight your battles alone. Don't let other Christians fight their battles alone. When you see someone struggling, and you know there is something you can do to help them, reach out in love. It may not always be inside of your comfort zone. There is room in the rescue boat for all of God's children.

HIDDEN BLESSINGS

*And seeing the multitudes, he went up into a
mountain: and when he was set, his disciples came
unto him: And he opened his mouth, and taught
them, saying, Blessed are the poor in spirit: for
theirs is the kingdom of heaven. Blessed are they
that mourn: for they shall be comforted.*

Matthew 5:1-4

It may not seem that being poor or in mourning is a blessing. Sometimes sad things teach us very valuable things. I am not saying that you have to be poor to be blessed. But, if you are poor, that will not keep you out of heaven, and it may even turn out to be a blessing in disguise.

Live long enough, you will have some days of mourning. Have comfort in knowing that God is there to get you through some very difficult times. Other people may come into your life, other opportunities may open up. This intricate mosaic of life and what happens next is something only God can orchestrate. It is a blessing that we don't have to figure out all of these things by ourselves. Over time, bits and pieces usually come together letting you know that God knows exactly what He is doing, even if we don't.

People try to explain bad news, but not usually very well. Only God can turn bad news into good news.

DO GOOD. BE BLESSED.

Blessed are the meek: for they shall inherit the earth. Blessed are they which do hunger and thirst after righteousness: for they shall be filled.

Blessed are the merciful: for they shall obtain mercy. Blessed are the pure in heart: for they shall see God.

Matthew 5:5-8

There is an old saying regarding people who do good deeds that they get punished for it. That is clearly not what the passage above says. Your blessings may not directly come from the person you helped, but I believe God will find a way to bless you in other ways.

There are times when it is a very good thing to be meek. Why argue over a point that is minor? Or why attack a person's character just because they won a game and you lost? There is a time and place for different ways to handle conflicts like confronting, retreating, compromising or ignoring. Different options for conflict resolution are there for a reason, including being meek. Pray and think before you speak, especially against someone.

Develop a hunger for righteousness so that it becomes second nature to you. Show mercy on others, because one day you may need them to show mercy on you. Have a loving heart and spirit. Let your love be on the inside and show on the outside.

LEARN HOW TO GET ALONG

Blessed are the peacemakers: for they shall be called the children of God.

Blessed are they which are persecuted for righteousness' sake: for theirs is the kingdom of heaven.

Blessed are ye, when men shall revile you, and persecute you, and shall say all manner of evil against you falsely, for my sake.

Rejoice, and be exceeding glad: for great is your reward in heaven: for so persecuted they the prophets which were before you.

Matthew 5:9-12

Getting along with others does not come naturally. You have to study how to do it. Practice it and believe that it is in your best interest. You may not get an instant reward. On the flip side, if you "flip someone off" by disrespecting them, bullying them, and doing other hurtful things, that can escalate into a very nasty fight.

Think twice, three times and four if you have to before saying or doing anything negative. Just because "you are right" and "they are wrong" doesn't necessarily mean you have to be the one to tell them. Sometimes there is a spiritual battle going on and before you know it you are in a fight with the Devil, all by yourself.

Rise above petty things that really reflect hidden insecurities on the part of the aggressor. Always remember that you have options which can bring you opportunities not currently known to you. Do you know how to use the option of being a peacemaker? If not, find out. If you do, practice your peacekeeping skills.

THE GIFT OF GRACE

The grace of our Lord Jesus Christ be with you all.
Amen.

Philippians 4:23

Christ's grace to us is a very special element in being a Christian. Through His grace we are forgiven of our sins and receive unmerited salvation. There would be no other way to get to heaven without it. His grace is truly a gift. It is a gift that brings us joy, peace, and love. There is no greater grace in the whole universe.

AMBASSADORS FOR CHRIST

But be ye doers of the word, and not hearers only, deceiving your own selves.

For if any be a hearer of the word, and not a doer, he is like unto a man beholding his natural face in a glass:

For he beholdeth himself, and goeth his way, and straightway forgetteth what manner of man he was.

James 1:22-24

How wonderful it is to confess your sins and believe that Christ is your savior. Many of us have walked down that church isle to join the church and be baptized. Now you are a full-fledged, listed-in-the-church-rolls Christian. Amen.

Of course you know that joining a church is just the beginning of your walk in faith. It takes more than words to show people who you really are. Unless you walk around with a name badge that says, "Christian so-and-so" people would not know if you are a Christian except by your actions.

People are watching you. Many times the people who are not Christians look to see, "What's the difference between you and a non-Christian?" You can't just preach to people all day. You should show them by your actions. There is an added benefit to that. You remind yourself too who you are, an ambassador for Christ who shows love, not just talk it.

ONE GOD

And God spake all these words, saying,

I am the LORD thy God, which have brought thee out of the land of Egypt, out of the house of bondage.

Thou shalt have no other gods before me.

Thou shalt not make unto thee any graven image, or any likeness of any thing that is in heaven above, or that is in the earth beneath, or that is in the water under the earth:

Thou shalt not bow down thyself to them, nor serve them: for I the LORD thy God am a jealous God, visiting the iniquity of the fathers upon the children unto the third and fourth generation of them that hate me;

And shewing mercy unto thousands of them that love me, and keep my commandments.

Exodus 20:1-6

Greed is greasy. It can lead to a slippery slope to hell. Many objects can be "other gods" like money, jewelry, career jobs, other people, and yourself. It is so nice to have money and other worldly benefits, but they should never come before God.

Take a moment and look around you. What have you surrounded yourself with? What's in your purse, wallet, room? Are they "taking over your life" more than Jesus? Give Him some time too. Nothing is more valuable.

CURSE NOT

*Thou shalt not take the name of the LORD thy
God in vain; for the LORD will not hold him
guiltless that taketh his name in vain.*

Exodus 20:7

It happens to the best of us. A slipped tongue that sounds funny at the time. Or it may be an utterance of anger or frustration. It is so common that it may sound strange to some people if you do not curse. It is even worse when you use God's name in vain.

He is to be reverenced. He deserves respect. Would you call someone that you loved one out of their name some culturally incorrect word? Of course not.

It is in the Bible, in case some people are confused about cursing. It is not an innocent little thing. The brain, including yours, hears such negative words and images and may accept the belittling of the person as real. It is not real. So speak the truth to God by at least calling Him in His right name in the right way. It is a very big deal.

REST IS REJUVENATING

Remember the sabbath day, to keep it holy.

Six days shalt thou labour, and do all thy work:

But the seventh day is the sabbath of the LORD thy God: in it thou shalt not do any work, thou, nor thy son, nor thy daughter, thy manservant, nor thy maidservant, nor thy cattle, nor thy stranger that is within thy gates:

For in six days the LORD made heaven and earth, the sea, and all that in them is, and rested the seventh day: wherefore the LORD blessed the sabbath day, and hallowed it.

Exodus 20:8-11

Did you know that people who do not get enough rest increase their chances of shortening their life? Rest is when the body gets a chance to restore itself. Resting during breaks at work has been found to increase productivity.

In a world where workers are connected to the workplace 24/7 through emails, text messages, and smart phones, it is very tempting to downplay the importance of rest.

Make a point of finding time to rest. Jesus rested. God rested. It can be done. My prayer is that we all can rest more. Of course, when we are not resting, my prayer is that we are having fun, serving others, or being productive in our careers. The message here is "balance."

PARENTS PROTECT

Honour thy father and thy mother: that thy days may be long upon the land which the LORD thy God giveth thee.

Exodus 20:12

A good parent protects their child from danger, like avoiding getting burned from a hot stove. A child must learn to honor their parent in a way that reflects each age and stage in life. Once a child grows up and marries, for example, varied ways of honoring parents may change.

While no parent is perfect, the reality is that some parents should not even be a part of the child's life, due to abuse or neglect. But there is still a way to honor your parents. As an adult, you can "honor" them by being an outstanding Christian who has risen above the horrors of the past by finding ways to love others and self.

You may need to forgive them. You may need to spend more time with them in their later years. Honoring your parents shows your children how to honor you.

When you look back on your life, let it reflect that you took the thought and the time to honor your parents. God will protect you and keep you from much harm because of it.

MAKE LIFE, DON'T TAKE LIFE

Thou shalt not kill.

Exodus 20:13

Millions of lives would have been saved, if people would have only followed the four little words in the above scripture. People who never read the Bible know that it is wrong. Yet it is like a plague in our communities and worldwide.

There are some solutions out there, including but not limited to: prayer, mentoring, enforcement of laws, formal education, morality, home training, employment, non-discrimination, gun control, mental health treatment; conflict resolution training, peaceful communications education, international diplomacy of peacemakers.

The need is great. We may not be able to stop all of the killings, but everyone should be doing something, if only making donations to non-profit agencies that are. God will accept any help you give to our society.

BITTERSWEET SEX

Thou shalt not commit adultery.

Exodus 20:14

Sex within marriage can be a very sweet experience to the couple involved. It is also as God intended it to be. However, having consensual sex outside of marriage with someone else's spouse is not pleasing to God. I do not have proof of it, but I suspect that it is bittersweet for the adulterer. If we truly believe that God has written His laws in our hearts, a guilty conscience can result in regret, self-condemnation, and depression. Some people have even committed suicide or been killed because of adultery.

Committing adultery is a sin that can be forgiven. It may seem good in the beginning, especially to risk-takers, but in the end, there are consequences, even if "no one" (but God) finds out. It can haunt the adulterer for the rest of his or her life. But like other sins, God can heal those hurting wounds too.

For some people adultery is a "weakness" that requires outside help. For others, it is a secret that they decide to take to their grave. But whatever "disposition" such a person takes, first take your burden to God. Of course, to avoid the whole nightmare, do not commit adultery in the first place. Many people have regretted doing this sin because of the aftertaste.

YOU CAN'T STEAL

Thou shalt not steal.

Exodus 20:15

This is a commandment not to take what is not yours. Let's just get a little "philosophical" here. If everything belongs to God, and nothing belongs to man, accept what He gives to us, "How can we steal, what God has not given to us?"

Stay with me on this. God gives and God takes away. Imagine that someone steals, say, $100 from someone's wallet. Then the next day, that same person has to pay an unexpected additional $100 on a utility bill. As another example, what if someone steals some jewelry worth $100 from a retail store (without getting caught). Then soon after, they accidentally break their eyeglasses and have to pay $300. There are gains and losses throughout every person's life. God will come out ahead in the end. So how can you really get away with stealing?

Of course, a common scenario is that a person steals something, gets caught and not only has to give the item back, but is found guilty of a felony and sent to prison. It may have been car wheel covers worth $1,000, but the thief loses $10,000 in lost wages due to imprisonment.

What about the guilt feelings? It may seem like the thief may not be remorseful. But we do not know their hearts which have been infused with God's laws. Most people know it is wrong to steal. If you are such a person, remember, that God can forgive this sin too. Learn from the lesson, so that you do not repeat it. Most people have stolen something. Ask God to forgive you. Pay the person stolen from or "society" back if possible and reasonable.

Like violence, society must take action to prevent thefts in the first place. Individuals must be taught this is not only wrong, but of no lasting benefit, because you can't steal from God.

WHY LIE?

Thou shalt not bear false witness against thy neighbour.

Exodus 20:16

Why would a person accuse someone else of something they did not do? Is it to protect oneself? It is to steal from someone? Is it to take revenge? Is it a joke, meant to be funny? Is it a bully tactic? There are probably a million reasons why people lie on others. But the central underlying reason is usually insecurity, whether imagined or real.

Of course God knows if you are telling the truth or not about your neighbor. If you confess you sin, He will forgive you. I can't say the same for society. There are numerous laws forbidding false testimonies, especially under oath that can result in perjury charges and prison sentences.

Many lies can be averted, if the person just thought things through ahead of time. What are your moral beliefs? What are the risks? Spend some time in your meditations with the Lord. Understand that it is quite "human" to lie under pressure or for self-preservation. Ask God to prepare you for the unexpected. And when you feel that urge to accuse someone of something they did not do, ask God to guide you and stop you from committing a sin. This is one area that can be greatly improved upon simply by introspection. Self-examine yourself, and ask, "Why lie?" By the time you come up with the answer, hopefully the urge to lie will be gone.

THE OPPOSITE OF JEALOUSY IS...

Thou shalt not covet thy neighbour's house, thou shalt not covet thy neighbour's wife, nor his manservant, nor his maidservant, nor his ox, nor his ass, nor any thing that is thy neighbour's.

Exodus 20:17

Talk about a sin that everyone has committed, from wanting another child's toy when a young toddler, to envying someone else's financial fortunes, this is it. Thank goodness for forgiveness. I am not going to go "deep" on you on this. Suffice it to say, that we all have some insecurities, whether it is about our bodies, bank account or brains.

If it will make you feel better, remember that God made everyone unique. You are who you are and have what you have for a reason. They can't be you and you can't be them. It is okay to admire and look up to people as a motivator for your own goals. You will not lose out on any of God's blessings, just because He has blessed others.

When you find yourself wanting what is not yours, you have options. You can belittle the other person to try to make them feel bad about what you secretly want. You can pretend to yourself that the item wanted is worthless. Or you can do the opposite of jealousy which is "compersion." It is when you feel joy and happiness for another person's joy and happiness. That can take the divine intervention of God for most of us to switch our emotions around so drastically. But it is possible.

Jealousy is an emotion deeply rooted in the unconscious mind. Like most emotions that react to environmental cues, it is automatic, which I refer to as "default thinking." You can override default thinking by being prepared for negative feelings ahead of time.

The biggest problem comes in admitting that we are jealous of something. We know we shouldn't be, but those feelings are there. So we deny that we are jealous. I once heard that a priest recalled after decades of hearing confessions, not one person confessed to being jealous. Since we all, in my estimate, have those feelings, put that on your "please forgive me Lord, for I have sinned" list.

Ask God to help you. But the least you can do is recognize it and not outwardly show acts of jealousy. You can change your thoughts, then say something the opposite like, "I am so happy for you." Smile now, as your friend rides off in his Bentley.

THE LAW IS LOVE

Master, which is the great commandment in the law? Jesus said unto him, Thou shalt love the Lord thy God with all thy heart, and with all thy soul, and with all thy mind.

This is the first and great commandment.

And the second is like unto it, Thou shalt love thy neighbour as thyself.

On these two commandments hang all the law and the prophets.

Matthew 22:36-40

Everyday we are faced with thousands of decisions. Which sock do we put on? What should we eat for breakfast? Should I take this route or that to work this morning? When it comes to your relationships, decisions get more complicated and numerous. What do I say to person A? Should I go with person B?

It is a blessing that some of those decisions are aided by the question, "Am I doing this in love?" The above scripture to love God and your neighbor is profound because it lays the blueprint to guide our decisions and structure our lives no matter how complicated they may be.

Love nurtures and allows self and others to grow and develop into wonderful human beings. Love is what keeps our civilization civilized, under any law. So the next time you have to follow the law, start with love.

WRITE THE WORD

I will stand upon my watch, and set me upon the tower, and will watch to see what he will say unto me, and what I shall answer when I am reproved.

And the LORD answered me, and said, Write the vision, and make it plain upon tables, that he may run that readeth it.

For the vision is yet for an appointed time, but at the end it shall speak, and not lie: though it tarry, wait for it; because it will surely come, it will not tarry.

Behold, his soul which is lifted up is not upright in him: but the just shall live by his faith.

Habakkuk 2:1-4

When God tells us something, it helps sometimes to write it down. This is not only for your benefit, but also for the benefit of others. What would the world be like, if no one in Biblical times stopped to write down God's Word, which is now referred to as, "The Holy Bible?"

There are so many people in today's world that God is speaking words of wisdom to. I would encourage you to share some of those words with others. Maybe it is a vision of hope for the hopeless. Maybe is it a warning to the wayward. Maybe it is just good news from the Gospels. You never know who will be reading and reaping rewards from your writings.

It is my prayer that those who read my books, including this one, will be inspired to reach new heights of personal fulfillment and help to make a better society.

GOOD-DOERS ARE BLESSED

*But whoso looketh into the perfect law of liberty,
and continueth therein, he being not a forgetful
hearer, but a doer of the work, this man shall be
blessed in his deed.*

James 1:25

When we do good work for God's glory, He will bless us. It is also our way of saying "Thank you, Lord." Not everyone will appreciate your good deeds. But God is the one who counts.

If you are liberated from the death of sin, through Jesus Christ's sacrifice, you should show your faith as a Christian by doing nice things. That is what being a Christian is all about. Otherwise, what is the point of sticking around as human beings on earth, if we served no godly purpose?

Fulfilling your purpose is your work assignment. When it is done, God will call you home. So get busy and take care of business while you can. Christians have much work to do. Thank you in advance for your service.

THE ULTIMATE BOSS

For he that is called in the Lord, being a servant,
is the Lord's freeman: likewise also he that is
called, being free, is Christ's servant.

Ye are bought with a price; be not ye the
servants of men.

I Corinthians 7:22, 23

There are nice bosses and mean bosses. There are smart bosses and dumb ones. There are pretty or handsome bosses and ugly ones. Our first bosses are our parents. Then there are the government bosses and business bosses. There are marriage bosses and church bosses. There are evil bosses and saintly bosses.

We also have "invisible" bosses. They are the bosses in our heads that tell us to do this or that. Which one do we follow? No one wants to follow the wrong boss. The Holy Spirit and *The Holy Bible* are excellent resources to guide us in following the ultimate boss, Jesus Christ. Let Him guide you on whom to follow or not.

HEAR IT?

*So then faith cometh by hearing, and hearing by
the word of God.*

Romans 10:17

There is a familiar saying that God gave us one mouth and two ears, because He wanted us to listen more than we talk. I have heard people get into fights because one person was not listening to the other.

It is human nature to want to be understood when we are communicating something important to us. But before the speaker can finish his or her sentence, the "listener" is too often speaking his or her position. This could have the effect on the speaker that the listener doesn't care what is being said.

God is like that. He wants you to listen to Him. If you don't, He may think that you don't care. When you listen to the other person, or God, and respond in a way the shows that you heard them, something very special happens.

You start to get a better understanding of what the speaker (God) is saying. With the greater understanding, you are more likely to see a point that you hadn't seen before. That is why your faith can grow from hearing the word of God. Next time you read your Bible, or hear a sermon, think about how that has affected your faith.

GOD'S GAME

But he said, Yea rather, blessed are they that hear
the word of God, and keep it.

Luke 11:28

To keep God's Word means to follow Christ's teachings. It means to be obedient. It is not enough to just hear the Word and then go on about doing things the way you have always done them.

Being a Christian is a participation activity. It is not a sit on-the sidelines, cheering and waving banners thing, then going home. It is about getting on the field and playing with your heart, mind and body to win.

In God's game, you are the key player for the game of your life. At the end of the day, you may have read the playbook, practiced ahead of time, heard the coach's instructions, and put on the best and coolest sports gear that money could buy. But until you run the field, swim the link, kick the ball, or make that slam dump basket (I know I am mixing apples with oranges in these sports metaphors), you are not playing God's game. You have to just do it.

GIVE TO THE POOR

Hereby perceive we the love of God, because he laid down his life for us: and we ought to lay down our lives for the brethren.

But whoso hath this world's good, and seeth his brother have need, and shutteth up his bowels of compassion from him, how dwelleth the love of God in him?

My little children, let us not love in word, neither in tongue; but in deed and in truth.

I John 3:16-18

If you are blessed enough to have more money and things than you need, give some of it to the poor. The Lord will bless you. It is a sad thing when super rich people want to take from the super poor. Fortunately, there are many millionaires who do share their wealth. Everyone can participate in giving, even if it is just a few pennies. It is Christian to love your neighbors, even the poor ones.

Love shows compassion. Wouldn't it be nice if people who had too much food shared it with people who are starving? It is a wonderful thing to hear that millions of people everyday do share some of their blessings with others who are down and in great need.

It actually feels good to help others. Not that you should expect something in return, but God sees every penny you have donated and blesses you for it. Continue to give and help others. The world will be a better place for your love.

A TRUSTED PATH

*Trust in the LORD with all thine heart; and lean
not unto thine own understanding.*

*In all thy ways acknowledge him, and he shall
direct thy paths.*

Proverbs 3:5-6

Trust is a test. Trust means that you are going to act and believe as though someone is going to live up to their promise, even if you can't make them. We trust people and things everyday. We trust that when we flip the light switch in our home, the light will come on. We trust that when we approach an intersection that the other driver will obey the traffic signals.

Trust God to help us to manage our lives. It is more risky to try to understand what to do all on your own than to trust God. He knows what went on at the beginning of the path, in the middle of the path, and at the end of the path. We can't always see what is around the corner of our lives. If you want to "Pave Your Life with a Purpose" as the motto goes for www.PaversHomes.com, you can only do that by trusting in the Lord. He knows the best trusted path for you to take.

GLORY TO GOD

Therefore let no man glory in men. For all things are yours; Whether Paul, or Apollos, or Cephas, or the world, or life, or death, or things present, or things to come; all are yours;

And ye are Christ's; and Christ is God's.

I Corinthians 3:21-23

It is true that individuals have accomplished amazing things on earth and in the sky. Some have climbed high mountains or swam deep into the oceans. Some have walked tight ropes, saved children from burning buildings and donated billions of dollars. People who have done great things should be recognized and honored, where appropriate.

But the only entity that should be glorified is God. It is a good thing to keep what man can do versus what God can do in perspective. The people in your personal life may seem bigger than God because they have financial, physical, or mental power over you. But keep in mind, all true power is in God's hand.

Many people have given up on their dreams because of the looming bigness of the image of an authority figure. It is like their minds are controlled by the person, even if the person is nowhere around or deceased. No person dead or alive should be more important than Christ. Listen and glorify Him above all others, because only He can save you.

CONFIDENCE GOD

It is better to trust in the LORD than to put confidence in man. It is better to trust in the LORD than to put confidence in princes.

Psalm 118:8, 9

Ever been defrauded by a con-artist? The whole scheme is for you to think, if "A" is true, then "B" is true. When the reality is that A may not necessarily lead to B. For example, you go on the website and find out a local person is selling a used copy machine. So you go to the person's home or business establishment and watch the copy machine working. You pay for it upon delivery and arrival to your house or business establishment. Since it worked at the other place, "A", you assumed that it will work at your place, "B." The only problem is that the machine didn't work at your place. But the con-artist is nowhere to be found or won't give you your money back.

Stay around the nicest person you know long enough and the chances are great they will disappoint you in something. But that is life. That is a lesson we learn as we grow in maturity. It is not the end of the world. It does not mean that you are stupid, or they are bad. It is usually part of human nature, especially when we think we will get something for nothing. (Stay away from strangers outside of a stadium offering to sell you a $25 gift certificate for $5.)

If we let all the people who have disappointed us get us down and keep us down, we could be depressed all day, every day. There is good news, however. God will not disappoint you. He will not offer you one thing and then switch it for something of lesser value. You can fall back on him and He will catch you every time. Forget the confidence man, and chose the Confidence God.

MAKE THY WILL MY WILL

I can of mine own self do nothing: as I hear, I judge: and my judgment is just; because I seek not mine own will, but the will of the Father which hath sent me.

John 5:30

There are times when we really want something a lot. We want it so much that all we can do is think about it. But something in us has a touch of uncertainty as to whether this is the best thing for us. So a Christian might ask God, "Okay, should I pursue this or not?"

If the Lord says, "No," what do we do? Do we try to convince Him to change His mind? Do we go ahead and pursue it anyway? Or do we follow God's advice? Of course, if God were standing right in front of us with a name badge on that reads, "The One and Only God," that decision might be easier.

Instead, more likely we will get an inner voice or a confirmation or, over time, the reason behind the Lord's decision. When you move ahead of something before you are sure of your decision, it may be too late to change your actions. There are ways to increase your awareness of God's advice. You can make a daily habit of reading the Bible, studying the Bible, reading devotionals, listening to sermons, attending Bible classes and just being still to "hear" from God.

But all that will not work, if you don't open your heart to Him who is able to keep you safe. Start by praying with an open mind that says, "Not my way, but thine, Lord," and mean it.

POTS WITH A PURPOSE

But now, O LORD, thou art our father; we are the clay, and thou our potter; and we all are the work of thy hand.

Isaiah 64:8

God does not make mistakes. When He made you, He made a beautiful person. If your self-image is anything less, remember God made you for a reason. When He created our world, he made us to fit right in. We are not outsiders in God's world.

Young children grow up to be teenagers who grow up to become adults. During their formative years, they develop a self-concept of who they are. It takes more effort for them to change the self-image as they get older. But if you feel any less than someone else, it is time to work on improving your "appearance." No matter how well you were raised, you still have to come to grips with not being as "good" as someone else in some specific area of human endeavors.

I think it is a good thing to accept your "imperfections," because it can remind you that you need God to get through life. I am reminded of a conversation I shared with some other people who had never gone to college. I was a college graduate. I told them that one of the things I learned in college was that I didn't know anywhere near everything, in fact, practically nothing compared to the vast knowledge that existed in the world. The second thing that I learned in college was that neither did anyone else.

Size, intelligence, connections, educational degrees, power, wealth, or positions do not make anyone better than you. We are all pots to God. I thank Him for making me a pot, which is a useful vessel. As long as your pot can carry God's Word, you are just as valuable to Him as anyone else in the world.

So hold your head up high. Walk with assurance. Speak with authority. You are a pot with a purpose! Hey!

OUTSMART YOUR BRAIN

Then said they unto him, What shall we do, that
we might work the works of God?

Jesus answered and said unto them, This is the work of
God, that ye believe on him whom he hath sent.

John 6:28, 29

We can talk ourselves out of practically anything if we do not believe it is possible. The brain is a funny thing when it comes to distinguishing between fact and fiction. Have you ever seen your brain? Unless there was a photo of it after you came out of anesthesia, it is not likely. But your brain sees you. Your brain sizes up what you can and cannot do. It may think you are too small or too big for that task. You have to outsmart your brain.

When the brain hears you say "I can't do..." or "I am afraid to do..." or "I will never do that..." it is hearing negative defeated thoughts that make it harder for you to overcome. However, in spite of what your brain thinks, if you maintain saying things like, "I can do this," or "I am doing that..." or "It is already done..." you can outsmart your brain into believing you can do what you previously thought you could not do.

What is it that you want to do for the Lord? Maybe it is something He has been asking you to do for many years, and your brain has talked you out of it. Start right now believing in God's ability to equip you with whatever He has asked you to do. Say and write positive affirmations about your goals. Before your brain knows it, you are doing great works.

LIGHT'S LESSONS

Ye are the light of the world. A city that is set on an hill cannot be hid.

Neither do men light a candle, and put it under a bushel, but on a candlestick; and it giveth light unto all that are in the house.

Let your light so shine before men, that they may see your good works, and glorify your Father which is in heaven.

Matthew 5:14-16

A little light can go a long way to remove darkness. No light is insignificant at night. Darkness is a symbol for sin. The lighted candle is a symbol for goodness and truth.

When it is dark outside, people often become afraid that more crimes will occur. It is like the criminal does not want to be seen, so they hide in the dark. But when the daylight comes with the sun, it brings hope for a brighter day.

One of light's lessons is to light a way for those who are lost in the dark to find Jesus. You can do this in so many ways. You can show love, forgiveness, reconciliation and peace. Start anywhere you can. The other light's lesson is when you light your candle, you tell the evil forces to stay away from you, because they do not like to see the light.

WHAT'S YOUR GIFT?

Now concerning spiritual gifts, brethren, I would not have you ignorant.

For to one is given by the Spirit the word of wisdom; to another the word of knowledge by the same Spirit;

To another faith by the same Spirit; to another the gifts of healing by the same Spirit;

To another the working of miracles; to another prophecy; to another discerning of spirits; to another divers kinds of tongues; to another the interpretation of tongues:

I Corinthians 12:1, 8-10

Paul wrote a letter to the church members of Corinth. Not everyone has the same gifts. However, everyone can be a witness for Christ by using their spiritual gift. Imagine a Christmas present in a festively wrapped box that is never opened. The giver would be disappointed. This year, remember to open your spiritual gift box, and use it.

DOUBLE DUTY

Bear ye one another's burdens, and so fulfil the law of Christ.

For if a man think himself to be something, when he is nothing, he deceiveth himself.

But let every man prove his own work, and then shall he have rejoicing in himself alone, and not in another. For every man shall bear his own burden.

Galatians 6:2-5

You are responsible for you. Whatever gifts and abilities God has given to you, use them to better your life, so that people do not have to do for you what you can do for yourself. At the end of you physical life, only you will have to answer for your behavior. The blame game doesn't work in heaven. What are you going to say when you approach the "pearly gates?" "Huh, the devil made me do it." Those excuses won't get you your wings. When you slip and fall in life, and you will, own up to your responsibility to admit that you sinned, not someone else.

In the same vein, you are to help your brother. Even as adults, we need each other. And other people need you. Look for them. They are there in need of your help. As I get older, I find that more and more people are reaching out to me for fellowship. I don't know what I can say or do to be good company, but I am trying very hard to at least, accept the invitations to meet. Maybe a word or two did help them with something I may have been totally unaware of. I have been blessed too by their words. So share your life with others. God made us a family. And family looks out for family.

GOD IS GOLD

If ye love me, keep my commandments.

John 14:15

If you love Jesus Christ, you will keep His commandments. That often means choosing between your fleshly desires and your spiritual goals. Commandments of love are there to protect you.

Yet people confuse what they want to do as better for them. I could write a book about such confusions and the consequences. For example, you want to eat that delicious looking and smelling dessert knowing it is over your daily calorie limit. Which is better? Eating the dessert, or saying "No thanks"? There goes your brain again, potentially getting you into trouble. The point is that what may seem good at the time, may be bad in the long run. This can be applied to so many decisions we make. All that glitters is not gold. God is gold. Love Him.

TAKE THE GOOD PATH

*My son, if thou wilt receive my words, and hide
my commandments with thee;*

*So that thou incline thine ear unto wisdom, and
apply thine heart to understanding;*

*Then shalt thou understand righteousness, and
judgment, and equity; yea, every good path.*

Proverbs 2:1, 2, 9

At the risk of repeating myself, and in this case it is worth repeating, study and listen to God's Word. The body may tell you one thing, but the Holy Spirit may tell you another. Learn God's commandments. Listen to elders who have been there and done that. Seek understanding, which doesn't seek you. Learn right from wrong so when you want to be righteous, you know what to do. Be fair, honest and just to others. You will go further in the long run.

And finally, after you have done all of the above, teach others to do the same. You have found a good path. Bring someone with you.

LOVE DOESN'T HURT

Charity suffereth long, and is kind; charity envieth not; charity vaunteth not itself, is not puffed up,

Doth not behave itself unseemly, seeketh not her own, is not easily provoked, thinketh no evil;

Rejoiceth not in iniquity, but rejoiceth in the truth;

And now abideth faith, hope, charity, these three; but the greatest of these is charity.

I Corinthians 13: 4-6, 13

Domestic violence is a terrible thing. One of the ways a person is able to continue hurting the victim is to make the victim think that she or he is loved by the abuser, so it must be the victim's fault. The victim, who is often in love with the abuser, takes on feelings of guilt, which further empowers the abuser.

Love is kind, does not go into a rage over excuses of jealously; doesn't belittle the other person, nor bully them. Love is slow to anger; and does not do evil acts of violence. Love seeks the truth in kind ways. Love does not laugh at someone else's misfortune. Love builds character, not tear it down.

Love is meant to feel good when received, not hurt.

JOINT PEACE

Let us therefore follow after the things which make for peace, and things wherewith one may edify another.

Romans 14:19

I have self-studied the field of peaceful relationships for many years. I have designed and taught several seminars on the subject. The principles are fairly easy to explain. Once the participants hear them, it seems like a light bulbs goes off into their heads. It's that simple.

One of the biggest barriers I think people don't give and have peace is because they don't want the other person to have it. Somewhere in their minds, if they can't have it, neither can you.

Peace brings people together. Peace is about relationships. If you don't want to have a good and loving relationship with someone, you surely are not interested in a peaceful one. So before you get into the study of peace, ask yourself, if you have peace and do you want to share it with this the other person or group? If the answer is "yes," you will have no trouble learning how to have joint peace.

SPIRIT TO SPIRIT

Jesus answered, Verily, verily, I say unto thee,
Except a man be born of water and of the Spirit,
he cannot enter into the kingdom of God.

That which is born of the flesh is flesh; and that
which is born of the Spirit is spirit.

John 3:5-6

It would be so nice to live in a perfect world where everyone is healthy and happy. But, of course, we do not. Over time, our bodies give out and things start going down hill. You know your story of regrets, regressions, and ruined memories. Work with what you have. Do the best you can.

There is more to your story. If it wasn't for being born of the Spirit, it is hard to imagine getting through some tough times. Imagine two parallel worlds. One is the physical that the eye can see and touch, and one is the spiritual that the usual senses can't confirm. Christians believe in a spiritual world, where angels and demons move around the earth, either helping or hurting humans.

The best example I can give of how this works is this, you are driving down the street on your way home from work. You want to take the expressway but, if it is crowded during rush hour, you wonder if you should take the street route. You get a sense in your spirit to take the streets this time, even though you normally take the expressway. When you get home, you find out on the evening news that the expressway had a water main break and was flooded, even though it was a dry, bright sunny day. Your spirit talked to the Holy Spirit who guided you in the right direction.

Some people may say that is hogwash. They may only be listening to the physical world. You don't have to take my word for it. You can try having your spirit talk to the Spirit and "see" for yourself.

AGE-OLD WISDOM

Make no friendship with an angry man; and with
a furious man thou shalt not go:

Lest thou learn his ways, and get a snare to thy soul.

Be not thou one of them that strike hands, or of
them that are sureties for debts.

Seest thou a man diligent in his business? he shall stand
before kings; he shall not stand before mean men.

Proverbs 22:24-26, 29

The Book of Proverbs is one of the wisdom books in the Bible. The above passage is pretty clear. The amazing thing is that it was written many centuries ago, yet it is just as relevant today as it was then.

Be careful who you hang around with. Many people are in jail for being with the wrong people in the wrong place for the wrong reason. Pick your friends carefully. You don't have to have a lot of friends to have fun.

Take care of business. Even if you are an employee for a large company, making good money, and expecting a stable working future, study finance and business anyway. Back then, in biblical times, people did not have the safety nets (financial assistance) that some countries in the world have today for their citizens. Don't assume that the same safety nets that exist today will be there for you. Save your money so that if you do have to make it on your own you are not starting from scratch.

STAY OFF THIS LIST

Now the works of the flesh are manifest, which are these; Adultery, fornication, uncleanness, lasciviousness,

Idolatry, witchcraft, hatred, variance, emulations, wrath, strife, seditions, heresies,

Envyings, murders, drunkenness, revellings, and such like: of the which I tell you before, as I have also told you in time past, that they which do such things shall not inherit the kingdom of God.

Galatians 5:19-21

What a list. If you are guilty of any of them, work on getting off of this list. You should know the things that are wrong, but in case you don't, there it is above. If you need help, seek it. God knows who is on the list and who got off, so hiding the list is a waste o time.

You can do this. We can do this. God can help us. Once you are off of the list, ask Him to help you to stay off.

THE BYE-BYE LIST

*Now I beseech you, brethren, mark them which
cause divisions and offences contrary to the
doctrine which ye have learned; and avoid them.*

Romans 16:17

Have you ever been around people that cause confusion? They can just ruin your day and life. Some people you are better off avoiding, if possible.

There are all kinds of diplomatic ways to avoid people. You can be polite and truthful, and still stay away from them. Make your list of how to say, "Bye-bye" in advance, so that you will be ready for them.

GOD'S SUPREME COURT

Dearly beloved, avenge not yourselves, but rather give place unto wrath: for it is written, Vengeance is mine; I will repay, saith the Lord.

Therefore if thine enemy hunger, feed him; if he thirst, give him drink: for in so doing thou shalt heap coals of fire on his head.

Be not overcome of evil, but overcome evil with good.

Romans 12:19-21

The typical court case is usually captioned like, Jones v. Smith. The first name is the Plaintiff, who brought the lawsuit, and the second is the Defendant, who is responding to the lawsuit. Some people don't even bother with taking people to court and just try to take vengeance out on someone that they perceived has harmed them. The result is more like, Evil v. Evil.

Before you take any hostile actions against another, ask God, if this is for Him to take care of. It is very difficult to restrain oneself from hurting another in certain circumstances, but it is worth getting God to deal with the problem first. Ask Him what you should do.

If possible, love and be kind to your enemies. No one but God can dispense justice like Him. He will do you right. He is the *Supreme Court of Justice*.